10 MAKE-OR-BREAK CAREER MOMENTS

10
MAKE-OR-BREAK
CAREER
MOMENTS

Navigate, Negotiate, AND
Communicate FOR Success

CASEY HAWLEY

TEN SPEED PRESS
Berkeley

Published in the United States by Ten Speed Press, an
imprint of the Crown Publishing Group, a division of
Random House, Inc., New York.
www.crownpublishing.com
www.tenspeed.com

Ten Speed Press and the Ten Speed Press colophon are
registered trademarks of Random House, Inc.

Library of Congress Cataloging-in-Publication Data
Hawley, Casey Fitts.
  10 make-or-break career moments : navigate,
negotiate, and communicate
for success / Casey Hawley.
     p. cm.
  Includes bibliographical references and index.
  Summary: "Identifies the ten most critical moments
in a person's career when the right word can make a
life-changing difference and provides communication
strategies for navigating them with clarity and
conviction"—Provided by publisher.
  1. Business communication. 2. Career development.
3. Success in business. I. Title. II. Title: Ten make-or-
break career moments.
  HF5718.H298 2010
  650.1—dc22
                                           2009050517

ISBN 978-1-58008-723-0

Printed in the United States of America

Design by Katy Brown

10 9 8 7 6 5 4 3 2 1

First Edition

Dedication

To my prayer partners who have implored God that I would not always say the first thing that comes to my mind and who have been successful most of the time, at least when I would listen. Special thanks to Frances Pastore, Mary Thomas, Belinda Stone, Ann Kieffer, Caroline Long, Joyce Johnson, Angela Mitchell, Teresa Gernatt, Carolyn Caswell, Sandra Robinson, Chris Reynolds, Cathy Russo, Joan Holsenbeck, Sharon Powell, Ginny Scruggs, and Debbie Howell. They have worn out their knees in prayer for me as I have learned the lessons I pass along in this book. Thank you.

CONTENTS

INTRODUCTION

There is a secret handshake in business. There are codes and passwords that allow some people to pass on to higher levels. Not knowing these door openers can hold you, as a professional, back from the career you deserve, no matter how smart you are.

The real challenge is that the secrets you need to know are not called passwords or handshakes; they are far more subtle than that. The secrets that can advance your career are the unwritten rules, regulations, and nuances of what to do, what to say, and how to approach situations that pop up along your career path. What do you say when you unexpectedly find yourself side by side with an executive who can offer you a job or promote you in your company? How do you meet a new committee or team and communicate with members in a way that makes them embrace your ideas from the very start? What is the best way to handle that job interview? How do you accept awards, honors, and promotions in a way that wins the affirmation of your peers and not their jealousy? What do you say when you suddenly find yourself in a conflict with a coworker? And perhaps most important, how do you ask for a raise?

10 Make-or-Break Career Moments defines these door-opening moments and shows you how to navigate them triumphantly. In this book, you will find strategies for fluidly and confidently responding to these critical moments that can make your path to success faster and easier. Not following these strategies can mean taking unnecessary detours along the way—and delaying your success. You could miss out on that all-important job opportunity or fail to be asked to be part of an influential team or focus group in your company. You might miss the opportunity to impress an executive who could offer you a role in a new project or offer you a great job recommendation. You might even appear less savvy, professional, and mature than you really are—and you don't want to misrepresent yourself that way. Communicating effectively in these crossroads moments will ensure that you leave a positive and powerful impression on all you encounter.

Nothing alters your path to success like the right communication. The right word said at the right time can propel your career forward; conversely, careless words blurted out in one of those ten critical moments can damage an influential person's view of you forever.

The one common thread that will run through your entire career is that your communication will always be the chief tool with which you will reach your goals: better jobs, great teamwork with colleagues, and effectiveness with the people you manage. You will be continually honing your communication at every level, becoming more polished and professional in choosing your words. This book is a fast-track tool to prepare you right now for the most important moments in your career.

The ten particular moments focused on in this book were chosen based on consultations and interviews with hundreds of professionals in all industries, small businesses, nonprofits, education, government, and even places of worship. In every type of employment, communication was valued as an indicator of how successful an employee would be. These ten moments are universal and highly important to the employee's success, whether you measure success by salary, position, career satisfaction, or your impact on other people.

You will probably experience all ten moments: certainly all that relate to the job search process, conflicts with others, awards and recognition, as well as being fired or resigning. These moments are career-changers—altering your circumstances and probably your income for better or worse, depending on how you respond to what is going on in that moment. Every situation is different, but this book allows you to discover what other people have found to be successful in similar moments. Based on my experience as a consultant for more than twenty years, I have distilled each great idea into practical suggestions. Finally, this book is a great primer for those who can only think of the right thing to say after the fact, when opportunities have passed them by, and they are left with regrets for what might have been. With the help of these proven strategies, you can be the person who says the right thing at the right time.

1

THE **FIRST MOMENT** YOU MEET AN **EXECUTIVE** OR **OTHER KEY** BUSINESS CONTACT

Who in a company receives the least positive feedback of anyone in the organization? The janitor? No. The CEO. The higher up you go in an organization, the fewer "attaboys" and acknowledgments you receive on a daily basis. Although managers and supervisors are generally conscientious about giving hourly workers and lower-level professionals positive feedback for a job well done, no one feels it is necessary to do that for the executives. Those who get this kind of feedback generally respond very well to it; why, then, don't we offer our higher-ups the same strokes?

Executives listen to information all day and deal with problems. Positive communication is in short supply some days. When executives are at social functions or even company receptions, they, like anyone else, would welcome hearing about what's going *right*, interesting observations, and breaking news from the community and their industry. When you realize this, you've got the basis for a model of what to talk about when you suddenly find yourself standing beside an executive at a company function or at an industry conference.

There you are, standing by the coffee urn or the cash bar, and suddenly you realize that the person standing next to you is a vice president from your company. Should you take the coward's way out? Tell yourself that he does not want to talk to someone of your lowly status and quietly edge away? Not if you are trying to advance your career. For all you know, the executive would welcome someone new to talk to and may be trying to avoid the same old crowd he hears from all the time. You could be just the person who will turn a tedious night into a refreshing experience for him.

Sometimes, when professionals are put on the spot to converse with an executive, they become desperate to say something— *anything*. Big mistake. An inexperienced conversationalist may say something that comes out as critical or shallow. Your response to the opportunity to make a great impression becomes pretty unimpressive.

So what can you actually say? Think M.I.S.S.I.O.N. possible! The M.I.S.S.I.O.N. model is a method to help you come up with timely conversation starters that will save you from just standing there with that deer-in-the-headlights look on your face as you struggle to come up with something to say. More important, it will guide you to positive topics, so you will have no regrets. A conversation with an executive is a wonderful opportunity for revealing who you are and the intelligence and creativity you can bring to her organization. The M.I.S.S.I.O.N. model helps ensure you make good use of that opportunity. You want to make sure that the meeting with you is memorable to the executive—in a good way. M.I.S.S.I.O.N. is a mnemonic—a memory aid consisting of letters that stand for key words. In this case, the letters will help you remember the following topics you can use to have a successful conversation with an executive:

THE M.I.S.S.I.O.N. MODEL

M = Milestones in projects
I = Individual contributions and experiences
S = Speeches, events, and articles that connect you
S = Self—as in *be yourself*
I = Interesting nuggets
O = Opportunities
N = Neighborly talk

M = Milestones in projects

Everyone congratulates the boss at the finish of a project. But you will be the exceptional person if you notice and comment on milestones along the way. A milestone is one step of many that must be accomplished between the beginning and the end of a successful project. Making a positive comment about a milestone that has been achieved on a long-term project says many complimentary things about you. First of all, it says that you noticed; therefore you are observant, unique, and perceptive, and you care about the company. It also says you are refreshingly different from all those who *haven't* mentioned it. You're the thoughtful one who's brought up this mini-success in a conversation.

Milestone events vary according to what your company is trying to achieve in any particular year. For example, if a company is trying to launch the sale of a new drug, some milestone events might include these:

- Passing initial in-house testing
- Gaining FDA approval
- Determining a name for the product
- Completing the marketing plan

After the launch, an executive will be hearing from everyone. Be among the handful who appreciates the significance of small successes along the way.

Here's another example: the establishment of a new subsidiary or branch or even a relocation of your company. The following are likely milestone events for such an opening:

- Selection of a site
- Board approval to move forward
- Groundbreaking
- Selection of an architect or builder
- Publication of related news articles

Ken Blanchard has had an extraordinarily successful career as a business author, motivational speaker, and thought leader. Much of his work, especially the bestseller *One Minute Manager*, is based on the quest to "catch people doing something right." His premise is that it takes no ingenuity to see and comment on what is going wrong. The extraordinary individual will hone the ability to comment on the things that are going right. In a world of "picture straighteners," the employee who can ignore the obvious complaints and criticisms, and instead offer intelligent observations about things that are going well, will shoot to the top. Such an employee will stand out from the crowd and be listened to by people at all levels of the organization.

I = Individual contributions and experiences

Denver resident Joe Ratway of Performance Advantage tells about an encounter with one of his personal heroes, Federico Peña, former secretary of transportation and former mayor of Denver. Joe happened to be on an escalator traveling parallel to the escalator Peña and his wife were on in the Denver airport constructed during Peña's time as mayor. Joe leaned across the handrails and, with a sweeping gesture to the magnificent airport, said, "Mr. Secretary, I just want to thank you for the legacy you gave me and all the citizens of Denver." Peña waited for Joe at the bottom of the escalator, introduced him to his wife, and engaged him in conversation. This conversation would never have taken place if Joe had not been presumptuous enough to speak up.

All of us like to be acknowledged for our individual contributions and experiences. Many executives have pretty healthy egos and respond well to concrete acknowledgment of specific accomplishments. For example, if you meet an executive who has recently been named chair of the local chamber of commerce, congratulate him. If you don't overdo the compliments, this will come across not as self-serving flattery but as simply good manners. It's always appropriate to congratulate executives who have recently been acknowledged in ways such as these:

- Elected to an office in any organization or charity
- Selected to serve on a board

- Given a noteworthy honor or award, like "Business-person of the Year"
- Promoted within your company
- Invited to speak at a visible industry or community event

Here are some other accomplishments you could acknowledge:

- A successful campaign to get legislation passed or ordinances changed that benefit your business
- An industry award or recognition
- Implementation of a program that the executive has always shown an interest in, such as a mentoring program or a technology change
- An award or recognition for the executive's company

When you mention an individual's contributions, it's critical to have something positive to say that is also specific and not just general fawning. Make it a practice to read about your company, your industry, and influential people in both areas. Read all of your company's newsletters, magazines, and prominent website articles. Read at least one trade magazine monthly. Also read one general business publication like the *Wall Street Journal* or a business magazine. If you read these on a regular basis, you will never be without something of value to contribute to an unexpected conversation.

Warren Buffett, legendary investor and CEO of Berkshire Hathaway, agrees that reading is the strategy to employ for success in communicating with business people—according to the independent Harvard weekly *Harbus*, in the article "My Pilgrimage to Omaha: The Great Warren Buffett Shares Personal Insights, Advice with Eager Group of HBSers" (January 23, 2006).

When asked for his advice to graduating MBA students, Buffett, who plays bridge with Bill Gates and poker with Alan Greenspan, said, "Read, read, read." He credits reading with not only the start of his career but also his current successes. Early in his career he would read the bound version of *Moody's* page by page, looking for undervalued companies. Today he is more likely to be reading the Korean *Standard & Poor's*, but the principle remains the same: read to look for opportunities in business.

If you handle your own accomplishments and goals tactfully and not boastfully, these can be conversation topics as well. No one likes a braggart, but we do like people who take joy and pride in their work. Do not hesitate to share your enthusiasm for company successes in which you played a part. Mention your contribution, but be sure to praise the company or department and not yourself. The following are examples of comments you could make to share a moment of success with an executive:

- "You know the SR-5 bill you recently helped get passed in the legislature? I was part of the team that did the market research on that. Congratulations."

- "I saw the new sales script you gave us for telephoning potential new customers in our community. I want to tell you that I think the new model will help us win more mid-size businesses. Even though we have only a three-person sales team at this point, I am very proud that I led the team in sales last year. I think I can sell even more using the new model."

- "I wanted to thank you for calling the president of Logitech for us. All of us who worked on that sale were excited about winning that account, and I think your call made a difference."

- "Did you see that our team in accounting received an A+ rating from the auditors? That should help us next year when we file our Sarbanes-Oxley report."
- "Do you remember when you asked all teachers who sponsor a team or extracurricular activity to trim their budgets by 10 percent this year? I just wanted to let you know that we will exceed that. We have been taking a hard look at some things, and I think we may actually trim our budget by 13 percent. It helped to have a target."
- "I know you were very active in the Cobb County Chapter of the American Institute of Banking early in your career. I was just elected treasurer. Any advice?"
- "On the Augusta Newsprint project, did you know that every member of our implementation team participated in making the recommendations the client liked so much? It was really one of the best collaborations I have ever been a part of; I learned a great deal about teamwork, and you can't argue with the results."

Don't mention how many hours you worked or that you did not finish some nights until 3:00 A.M.; there is nothing impressive about drudgery, and you will sound as if you are whining. Just show your joy in a job well done and give credit to the executive, the team, the company, and finally yourself. Show you have a stake in the company by taking pride in its successes and recognitions. Don't brag, but demonstrate that you were a fully engaged part of the team that brought a project to a successful conclusion.

Donald Trump recently met an audience member as he prepared to tell his rise-and-fall story at the Real Estate and Wealth Expo *in Atlanta, Georgia. He pointed to a casually dressed person in the front and asked him if he knew the story. The person said he did, so Trump told him, "Tell the story." Unknowingly, Trump invited a motivational speaker onstage. In that moment, Orrin Hudson "was hired."*

Anyone having watched the popular show The Apprentice *understands how tough Donald Trump can be as a thriving businessperson. In the Apprentice reality show, he gives two opposing groups a challenging task and watches them over the course of the project. At the end of each show, he grills each team on their performances and ultimately decides who continues on the show. For those who do not make it, Trump utters the blunt words, "You're fired!"*

The passion that Trump has about being successful is similar to the message Hudson routinely relays to kids. Naturally, Trump was impressed with Hudson's delivery and promised to call him. With the crowd buzzing, Hudson told The Chess Drum *that streams of attendees came forth to praise him on his impromptu presentation. Perhaps most in the audience were not familiar with the Hudson story. However, Hudson's story is fairly well-known. His numerous interviews and articles have been featured on major TV stations, newspapers and websites (more than a dozen on* The Chess Drum*).*

Most recently Hudson was the subject of an article on the front of the Lifestyle section in the March 4th [2007] edition of the Atlanta Journal-Constitution. *The story highlighted the efforts Hudson has made in the lives of youth, including that of Aaron Porter, a 6'5" eighteen-year-old who had incurred serious charges of juvenile misconduct (including an attempted murder of his father). Porter met Hudson and received enough inspiration and coaching that he won the first annual Georgia Association for Alternative Education (GAAE) state-wide chess championship.*

(www.thechessdrum.net/newsbriefs/2007/NB_OHudson2.html, March 7, 2007)

S = Speeches, events, and articles that connect you

If there are truly six degrees of separation between each of us and every other person on the earth, then there should be only a few degrees between you and any executive you meet. After all, you are both in business and success oriented. The obvious connection between you and the executive in front of you may be surprisingly easy to talk about: it is the event or speech you are attending. What brings the executive there? What brings you there? Are there commonalities?

SPEECHES. If a speech or presentation was made, a great topic of conversation is to pick out a specific point the speaker made and discuss that with the executive. If you make a generalization like "Good speech" or ask a generic question like "What did you think about the speech?" you may actually be putting the executive on the spot. Plus, it comes across as rather unimpressive to make a comment that reflects no discernment or thoughtful observation on your part. You are in no way demonstrating your intelligence or industry knowledge with such a statement.

Instead, choose a noncontroversial but interesting point the speaker made and discuss it with the executive. Don't put the executive on the spot by asking about a divisive issue, or she may make her excuse to get away at the first opportunity. You should offer an observation first and then open up the discussion for the executive to contribute. Here are some examples:

- "I thought her comparison of changes in our industry to the changes in the banking industry in the eighties was interesting. What was your take on that?"
- "She made a strong case for departmental branding. I am still undecided about the value, though. What is your perspective on that?"
- "I thought the strongest point in his argument was the long-term cost containment. You have a much broader perspective on that. What do you think?"

EVENTS. When you meet an executive for the first time, look at the context of the encounter. Is it a conference, a meeting of a professional association, a social reception, or a departmental meeting? The context itself is common ground for you and the executive. Find a conversation topic that relates to the event. The table on page 16 lists some suggestions.

ARTICLES. Executives may show up in print in a variety of ways. They are often quoted in newspapers, magazines, newsletters, and books. Some of them write for industry publications or professional journals. Do a search and find out whether the executive you want to talk with has been mentioned in print. The business librarian at your local university is the best choice to help you—and probably won't care whether or not you are enrolled. (Your local librarian is a good second choice for a resource.) If you plan to casually mention

IF THE EVENT IS A . . .	YOU MIGHT TALK ABOUT . . .
Conference	The conference topic, specific speaker, the executive's topic or field
Convention	Hot trends in the industry, companies who have a strong presence, vendors who have impressive booths, interesting and relevant people you have met at the convention and specific industry-related comments made
Professional association meeting	Regulatory changes, legislation that may affect your profession, offices the executive has held in the organization and questions about that experience, advice on higher education or certifications and their value to your career
Departmental meeting	The reason for the executive's being at the meeting, his expertise, how to learn more about the topic of the meeting, offering to supply information or to follow up on something the executive expresses interest in, the history of the executive's relationship with the department or with the department head ("How long have you known Barry Steiner?" "Have Barry and you worked together in the past?")

an article that features the executive's name, be sure it is a positive article. You don't want to bring up an article that is a sore spot with the executive.

Be sure you thoroughly read any article the executive has written. Prepare two "softball" but intriguing questions. These questions should be easy enough that you won't risk embarrassing the executive but still thoughtful enough to reveal your own intelligence. Softball questions will not put the executive on the spot by asking him to answer controversial questions or asking for such fine detail that you force the executive to say, "I don't know."

Bring the questions up in a casual way, for example:

- "I see in the *Journal* that you were quoted as saying you think housing starts will pick up in the spring. Do you continue to be encouraged?"
- "That was an interesting article about you in the *Journal* last week. I didn't realize that you had spent time in Australia. When were you there?"
- "Those statistics you quoted in the *Journal* last week were impressive. Did our research department come up with that 23 percent figure, or is that an industry projection?"

Whether you are going to attend a conference, a departmental meeting, or a 10K race, the one thing you must do is prepare to make a memorable and positive impression. You want the executive to return to the office next week and say, "I met a pretty impressive up-and-comer last week. Let's keep our eye on this one for the future."

How do you prepare to rock the executive's world? Before you attend an event, take the following steps:

- Study the agenda and descriptions of any speakers or events. Know what you will be doing, including your schedule and objectives, from the moment you arrive. You will appear savvy and collected.
- Google the leaders who will be there—especially those you hope to impress. Executives don't like for you to

waste their time, so be knowledgeable about who they are and what their current interests are before you go. Use every possible avenue to learn about them: ask their employees about them or people who know them from any area of their lives.

I interviewed an executive with Morgan Stanley who insists that it's not what you say but knowing whom to say it to. He attributes much of his success to a sponsor or mentor who gave him great advice about how to talk with people with the power to hire or promote him. His sponsor was committed to selling him internally, and the aspiring executive saw his own job as making it easy for the sponsor to do that by following his advice. Now that he himself is finally an executive, he says he finds it really amusing that when people meet with him, sometimes he can tell that they have been coached; someone has told them, "Here is what the director will want to talk about and here are the questions you should be prepared to answer." He rather likes it. He compares the prepared people favorably to the people who are not even familiar with him or what his company does. The executive's final advice: "Find someone in the organization who knows who is who and let that person advise you. Then listen."

■ Be familiar with the hottest topic that will probably be discussed at the event. If it is a conference on a specific topic, familiarize yourself with it a bit by researching it through the EBSCO online research database or other online tools. Or, if there is breaking news in your industry, go to news websites—try the major networks and news services such as CNN.com or Fox.com—so you will have something to offer if you get into a conversation with your executive idol.

- Just before entering the event, focus—not on yourself, but on the information you have and on the other attendees. By all means do not focus on yourself (for example, thinking only of what you are going to say, how you look, or the way you may come across); that leads to feeling nervous, and then you risk coming across as scatterbrained and boorish. Go into an event with the intent to find someone fascinating, no matter how hard that may seem. Listen intently and scout for something of interest or value to respond to.

- Don't be task oriented, thinking only of the tasks you want to accomplish in these moments. Professionals move beyond tasks and are open to surprising or being surprised by others. Be a sponge, ready to soak up ideas and people. Don't see everything through the lens of your own job and your department. Try to view the company the way the executive does: with a macro, not a micro, view. That means thinking about your company as it relates to the industry, the community, and legislative bodies. However, be prepared to come down from that high perspective and answer specific questions about your job. You may be just the person to offer some answers the executive really wants to know.

- In most cases, keep the conversation light. Managers and executives go to these events to be informed but also to have some fun and enjoy getting out of the office. If you trap your contact into a deadly dull conversation and question her as if she is defending a dissertation, she will not enjoy meeting you and will certainly plan not to meet you again. And if you run into an executive at your neighbor's housewarming, remember that she deserves a night off. Don't make it all about work.

If, however, you know the executive's company is about to launch a corporate blog, there's nothing that says you can't bring up blogging and see where the conversation leads. If she bites, you might mention blogs you have read that relate to her industry. Or you might point out innovative techniques and applications of blogs so that she becomes interested in what you have to say. She may even want to continue the conversation the following week, in her office or over lunch.

- If you work in the same company but the executive doesn't know you, be sure to introduce yourself and tell the executive which department you work in. Also, mention any interesting or high-profile projects you are a part of. Being interested in your work is a winning quality; it makes you more interesting. Just the fact you work in the same company will probably be all that is needed to start the conversation.

- Be sure to connect if you work for different companies but in the same or related fields. For example, you could say, "Hello, Arnold; I understand you are in marketing for Coke; I am in marketing at a midsize local firm." If he responds, you might want to offer that you are in brand management and ask whether that is part of his department, or you might mention a recent marketing coup Coke has accomplished.

S = Self—as in *be yourself*

The one piece of advice that almost every executive gives regarding meeting and talking to executives is this: be yourself. This, they all agree, is the foundation for making a good first impression. Today there are many words for this quality—authenticity, transparency, ethical clarity—but they all mean the same thing. Don't try to appear more intelligent or experienced or knowledgeable than you actually are—just be yourself. The pursuit of knowledge is good, and preparing and studying for events will pay off, but don't try to put a veneer over what you really are. Surprisingly, many executives like the idea that the job seeker or less-experienced professional is something of a blank slate, and they don't mind sharing their stories of success and bits of advice. And executives have had years of experience in recognizing phonies and shams. "Fake it till you make it" will not work here; these discerning executives will see through you in about two minutes. But executives find it very winsome when a less-experienced person is honest about where she is in her career and asks for insight and wisdom.

Kevin Fletcher, vice president of community and economic development for Georgia Power, says this:

> *Don't try to be something you are not. Sometimes I speak on college campuses and business students come up to me with a corporate air and try to show me what savvy businesspeople they already are. They often try to sound as if they are highly experienced. I know where they are in their careers, and I know they don't have the experience. It would be much better to just tell me honestly a little bit about themselves and their lives thus far. I am genuinely*

interested in talking to people like that and find myself
enjoying their company. These are the people who make a
good impression on me.

I = Interesting

Executives are just regular human beings, interested in many
of the same things that interest other people. The same skills
that will make you an interesting conversationalist in other
areas of your life will make you interesting in conversations
with executives. Don't limit your conversations to just your
company or the executive's area of the company. They hear
about that all day long. Be up on the most current news in
general business, and extend your interest to global business.

The conventional wisdom is for sales representatives to
study the company website of the executive they are calling on.
One of the most successful sales executives in the technology
field, Frank Massengill, says he goes beyond that narrow scope.

What am I going to do, go in there and tell him about
his company? No—that's not interesting to him, and he
knows more about it than I do. Instead, I read about break-
ing industry trends and projections. I read about people
who are making news in their industry and ask him about
them. If I call on IBM, I might ask the executive what he
thinks about a decision Michael Dell has made recently.
They really enjoy talking about that, and it makes them
want to have more conversations with me. I make sure
that I have researched enough that I have something to
contribute so there is value in talking to me. Gradually,
I gain credibility and the executive's confidence so he is
receptive to me.

Angela Strickland, director of energy efficiency and conservation for Georgia Power Company, agrees that keeping current "gives you something of interest to talk about." She has breaking news alerts sent to her BlackBerry by the *Atlanta Business Chronicle.* Your local business newspaper or general interest newspaper probably has the same service. In addition to her industry education and experience, Angela credits her comfort with executives, in part, for her fast advancement at a relatively young age in one of the largest electric utilities in the United States. She regularly meets elected officials of her state and top executives in her industry. She is always informed about her industry as well as events taking place in her state and community. Angela suggests bringing up a front-page story and then asking the executive what impact, if any, the event will have on the executive's industry or company. She also suggests the following questions to engage executives in a more personal conversation meant to build relationships:

- Where did you go to college?
- What was your first professional position?
- What was your first job in your industry?

O = Opportunities

Executives love talking about opportunities: opportunities for new revenue streams, opportunities for growth, opportunities for saving on money, labor, or other resources.

If you scratch the surface of most any executive, you will find a futurist hidden beneath the well-tailored suit. Executives are chosen, in part, for their abilities to see beyond the obvious and the status quo. They have often distinguished themselves in leadership, initiative, visionary thinking, and creative problem solving. They were able to exceed expectations in roles as individual contributors and first-line supervisors. Taking an existing organization and advancing it to the next level is part of their success path. For reasons like these, they usually respond well if you engage them in conversations about opportunities:

- Where do you think are the best new opportunities for revenue?
- What are some new products consumers would like to see from our industry?
- What opportunities might [this event] create for our industry? (Base this question on current news like the oil crisis or import/export legislation.)
- What areas of our company or industry do you think are the growth areas?
- Are there industries that support ours that will be growing over the next decade?
- If you were in my role, what would your advice be?

Not all executives are creative thinkers, but if you have the chance to speak with one who is, she will enjoy these future-oriented conversations immensely.

N = Neighborly talk

If you are talking to a local executive, then you have something very important in common: your community. Community events, new construction, the arts, transportation, and many other community factors affect both your life and the executive's—instant common ground. If you know the executive is involved in the local opera or PTA or whatever, bringing up these topics may spark his interest.

CREATE YOUR OWN EVENTS
AND OPPORTUNITIES

Today, Amy Kwon is the innovative founder of Signature Sweets by Amy, creators of fantasy theme cakes for very special events in the corporate and social world. Before starting her own business, Amy had an extraordinarily successful career as a manager in a health-related nonprofit organization. Amy created opportunities for herself whenever she attended any work-related event.

A turning point in her career in the nonprofit arena was the day she attended an annual off-site meeting. Amy chose to rise early one morning and join a walking group that the meeting organizers listed as an optional activity. On that walk, Amy was able to get to know the chief operating officer of her company, someone she ordinarily would not have much exposure to. More to the point, the COO was able to get to know Amy and found her credible. Later, when Amy needed support for an important initiative her department was undertaking, the COO offered that support because the initiative was the right thing to do and she trusted Amy. The brief encounter had helped build that trust.

Amy's advice on meeting executives is, "Don't be shy. Everyone wants to meet new people, so step right up and introduce yourself." Many young professionals have found that the 10K runs, the walk-a-thons, and the corporate gym have offered them a way to level the ground between themselves and top executives. If you are a young IT professional and are biking across your state with your CIO, you will have an opportunity to get to know the executive in a way you never would have in the office.

Of course, sports and recreation events are not the only ways to get to know people who can help your career. Almost every executive is involved in one or more charities. Charities are always looking for volunteers. Voilà! You are a volunteer, and as such you are a valued part of something that has significance to the executive. The all-for-one-and-one-for-all camaraderie that pervades most volunteer activities gives you the potential for exposure to the executive. And you do some valuable work for the community at the same time.

As you work with an executive—perhaps helping to plan an event, or distinguishing yourself by selling the most memberships for the chamber of commerce when he is leading the membership drive—you are building relational capital. Working together toward a mutual goal outside the company will showcase skills you have that could be used inside the company. An executive may take notice and think of you the next time a new role needs to be filled with your skills set—even if it's several levels above your pay grade. Such obstacles are not insurmountable for an executive.

Kevin Fletcher became an executive in a conservative, traditional utility company at a very young age—a real feat. He is perhaps the most relational executive in the utility industry today, demonstrating interpersonal skills that have brought him accolades from business people from Macon, Georgia, to Hong Kong. When he meets new people, Kevin says he always asks them where they are from. That one question often leads to all sorts of topics, including family. Although you must be careful not be too personal or invasive when you ask about family, simply asking where people are from allows them to tell you as much or as little about themselves as they want. The question is also open to interpretation. Some people will tell you about their roots. Others will proudly tell you about the posh suburb they live in or the transitional neighborhood they are helping revitalize. You never know when you are going to discover a new neighbor. And wouldn't it be an added bonus if the neighbor is an executive who becomes an advocate?

OPPORTUNITIES FOR USING THE M.I.S.S.I.O.N. MODEL

Brush up on the M.I.S.S.I.O.N. model just before you attend any of the following events:

- Company functions that allow time for refreshments and conversation. Some of these events take place before or after a speaker.
- Retirement and promotion parties. Most executives have formed connections along the way with employees at all levels and will stop by these events to say congratulations.
- Professional meetings and trade show events. After all, you are in the midst of many decision makers who need people with your experience.
- Events outside the office that are attended by many people in your company: golf tournaments, races and walks, charitable occasions, civic and community events.

If you are on a mission to build career credibility, begin practicing the M.I.S.S.I.O.N. model on friends and associates at lower levels of the organization. You will be surprised how easily you will be able to apply the model to that unexpected conversation with an executive or key business contact when the time comes.

GAMES *NOT* TO PLAY WITH AN EXECUTIVE

It's horrifying to see an up-and-coming, well-meaning employee sabotage his own career by trying one of the following approaches to impressing an executive. These do not work. Do not try these in your home company or anywhere else. Not only will the attempted gamesmanship in these tactics fail to inspire an executive to advance your career, but you will probably wind up on his personal "do not call" list. Although it might be tempting to prove your intelligence by upstaging the executive with your superior knowledge, a more successful communicator will walk the line between drawing attention to her achievements and seeming arrogant.

Who's the smartest person in the room?

This game was taught to you from your earliest elementary school years, so it seems unfair that it is suddenly unwise. In elementary school, you were encouraged to be the first kid with your hand in the air and to know all the answers. You were rewarded for that behavior for twelve years. You even got extra points for knowing things others didn't, and you were encouraged to demonstrate that to your teachers. In many ways, young people are encouraged to do this in college and in the competitive race to get into grad school. However, competing to be the smartest person in the room at a cocktail party or annual meeting just makes you appear obnoxious, especially if you are trying to prove the point in a ten-minute window with your favorite executive. Be realistic about what you can accomplish. Follow the golden rule of being more interested in others than yourself, and work in any conversational references to yourself gracefully. Only after expressing interest in the executive's company or other interests should you offer any nugget about yourself. If the executive mentions that she is thinking of using a blog to communicate with customers, you should take two actions. First, acknowledge what she said with a comment like "I can see that a blog would be very practical and effective for a local CPA firm like yours." Second, bring up your experience: "I have developed a blog for my college fraternity, and we were actually able to plan our entire ten-year reunion with it. Blogs are a great way to communicate with a large group that has something in common."

Don't drive the conversation relentlessly to topics that showcase you. Don't jump in too soon with the right answer or the pithy comment. Wait until the executive fully finishes a sentence, then pause for two seconds before speaking. Often, the executive will go on speaking and think you are extremely thoughtful in the way you listened so profoundly.

James M. Caswell, visionary real estate developer and founder of Habersham Partners, says, "I won't hire someone who is cocky. If I am hiring them, I have something to teach them rather than their teaching me." Caswell goes on to advise less-experienced careerists to be humble above all else in conversations with executives. This brilliant man, who has always seemed to have a knack for shrewdly predicting what office space and other commercial projects to build and where to build them, lives up to his own standards. In a thirty-minute interview, he mentioned at least six people he admired and gave them credit for his success. He enthusiastically admired one executive for his creativity, one for his generosity in opening doors for him with John Portman and other architects and developers, another for his profound intelligence, and still another for his ability to amass valuable land. Despite probing questions urging him to tout how he became successful, Caswell at no time took personal credit for the real estate successes in his career. Instead, he said, "I have never met a self-made man. Other people helped me, and that is true of every successful person I have ever met."

Take that as a cue. Allow the executive to tell you a principle or fact, even if you want to jump up and demonstrate that you already know it—perhaps even better than the executive does. Proving you are smarter than someone you want to mentor you is not a winning strategy. Despite having a reputation for impeccable integrity and legendary honesty, Caswell says, in situations like this, "Humility is the better choice, even if you have to feign it for a moment."

Twenty questions

In an effort to show interest and engage the other person, some career people ask one question after another. This relentless barrage of questions backfires. Instead of seeming genuinely interested, the questioner appears to be manipulative and the questions contrived. You should allow plenty of time for response and discussion after each question. When you're the questioner, be responsive to the answer; this is conversation at its best. Questions thrown at an executive like machine-gun fire can seem more like a grilling than a conversation with an enjoyable person who might be good to have around in the long term.

Stump the band/executive

In this game, the employee spends time dreaming up the hardest or most outlandish question he can possibly think of to ask the executive. Why would anyone be so crazy? Often, the questioner is trying to distinguish himself and make a memorable impression. He does, but it is not a good one. Or the questioner may be trying to demonstrate how smart he is to have thought of such a deep, profound question. Whatever your motivation, don't go there.

Investor Warren Buffett of Berkshire-Hathaway says, "You do not need to be a genius to be successful in business. If you have an IQ of 170 . . . you're probably best off selling 45 of those points to the highest bidder. What is most important is knowing the limits of and operating within your circle of competence—the range of personal skills and strengths you are able to use to give yourself an edge in the market." (*Harbus*, January 23, 2006)

Trivia

Mid- and lower-level employees give executives way too much credit for knowing everything. Executives often are great leaders and idea people, but may not know some of the facts you might think they would. Crafting a question about crass operating details can lead to an ugly moment. Stay away from minutiae; think big picture.

Ol' buddy, ol' pal

In a mistaken attempt to appear casual and unrattled in the presence of an executive, some people take it too far and treat the executive with an inappropriate level of familiarity. The executive is still a professional acquaintance, several levels above you in ranking. Some deference and respect is due. Don't cross boundaries that only personal friends would cross. These boundaries may relate to subjects like family and personal life or may involve personal space or touching on the arm or back.

Politics, religion, gender, and addiction

You cannot assume what a person's politics or religion may be, so avoid topics such as religion on a first encounter. And no matter how well-intentioned the comment may be, generalizations about gender or sex-related comments can be viewed as sexist. Sexist remarks can include comments about women loving to shop or gay men having good taste or all men being sports fans. Just avoid categorizing people like this.

Politics, religion, and gender are obvious topics to stay away from, but there is another category these days: lifestyle and addiction-related topics. Gone are the days when people laughed good-naturedly at the drinking excesses of celebrities like Dean Martin. The tragic declines of people like Britney Spears, Tiger Woods, and Lindsay Lohan make reality pretty gritty. More important, it is rare to find a family that has not been touched by some kind of addiction: gambling, pornography, drugs, alcohol, or whatever. It is not funny when you have watched family members or friends waste opportunities and surrender their lives to addiction. You could be considered insensitive and lacking in judgment if you make light comments about any type of addiction. Worse, the fact that you bring up alcohol or similar subjects can plant the seed of doubt about your own habits. No one needs an addictive personality as part of the team. The suggestion that you may have your own addiction issues could damage your prospects for inclusion in a team or project. If you avoid these pitfalls, you can leave the encounter knowing you have made a positive impression and built a link between you and an executive who could perhaps be influential in your career.

CLOSING OUT AN ENCOUNTER WITH AN EXECUTIVE

What happens after you ask these executives great questions to engage in conversation? How do you gracefully exit? Amy Kwon, who has worked primarily in the nonprofit industry, which fosters lots of networking—offers these two suggestions:

- Don't linger too long. You can make your exit with a handshake and a "Nice meeting you."
- Remember to exchange information with the executive by offering your card. You want this to be a contact for the future.

If you are in a traditional, legacy company, you may not want to ask directly for the card of an executive several levels above you in your own company. Offer yours and hope that the executive reciprocates. Pay attention to the executive's response—both verbal and nonverbal—after you ask a question or bringing up a topic. If you see he is uncomfortable or uninterested in talking about a topic, move on. Some people try to force the question, thinking maybe the executive just didn't understand it; that is rarely the case. Go to Plan B.

NO LOOKING BACK

With the encounter behind you, don't be self-critical. Sometimes, after a spontaneous meeting with an executive superstar, you may be tempted to pick apart everything you said and regret the brilliant things you forgot to say. Not only is this a waste of energy, but it is probably not valid. Some executives will not give you a clue whether you have made a worthwhile impression—so don't expect verbal validation at the end of the conversation. (If you get one, go ahead and privately celebrate!)

Visionary Apple cofounder Steve Jobs is famous for not appearing warm or responsive during a first encounter (though insiders say once you get to know him he can be a great guy). Depending on whose blog you are reading, a chance meeting with Jobs may be described as an instant connection with the extraordinary cofounder of Microsoft and founder of Apple; however, occasionally these blogs describe Jobs as rude, abrupt, and nonresponsive. Is the difference with Jobs or with the take of the young idol-worshippers that meet him? What they take away may be more valuable than they realize. Take, for example, Shel Israel's blog *ItSeemsToMe*, in which he shares the following story:

> *I had a similar encounter with a younger but equally ungracious Jobs in 1980, after he was keynote speaker for an event sponsored by the long defunct* The Executive *magazine. It was the first time I heard the "computers will change the way we work, play, and communicate speech," which was prophetic and inspirational to me. Afterwards, I waited outside for him in a cold December rain and*

when he left the building, I rushed up to him and told him that his talk had inspired me, that I had gone through a period where I had lost direction in life and that he had given it back to me. I wanted to join Apple and spread the word of the promise of his computers to humanity.

He stared at me for a second then asked me what I did for a living. I stammered that I loved to write, and right now I was working for a PR agency until I could find something meaningful. "My PR flack is Regis McKenna," he snapped more than a little impatiently. "Go work for him."

In fact, that's exactly what I did. But I never really worked much on the Apple account. As it turned out, that was a good thing. And I learned something about Jobs that seems to be true all these many years later. He's much more appealing when he's standing in front of five hundred people than he is close up.

(Shel Israel, ItSeemsToMe, August 2005. http://seems2shel
.typepad.com/itseemstome/2005/08/close_encounter.html)

Though some executives are much more admirable from afar, I wonder if Israel is being fair to Jobs in this case. I'd say that Jobs was actually being quite generous and genuinely helpful, even if his manner and his choice of words were brusque—it was cold and rainy, the man was in a hurry, and he'd had many experiences of being waylaid by eager aspiring employees. From my perspective, here are the takeaways Israel got from the meeting:

- To be given the name of Steve Jobs's PR guy is a huge gift to a young writer. Jobs didn't give general advice like, "Go to work for one of the larger PR firms." He gave Israel a *name*! That's huge!

- Can you imagine calling Regis McKenna and saying, "Steve Jobs told me to call you"? What a door-opener, considering Jobs had no evidence of the quality of the young man's work! Again, even some of our friends and associates won't open doors this way, but Jobs did this for a total stranger.

- What impressed me most about this story is that, as deluged as Jobs was in that moment, he stopped and really looked at the young man (thoughtfully, one might assume) and then asked him a question to get to know him a bit. Again, Jobs acknowledged the uniqueness of the person in front of him and did not give a generic answer. He went to the heart of what could be of specific value to probably the umpteen-millionth jobseeker who had confronted him that month. The personalized and meaningful advice Jobs gave was far more valuable than a feel-good moment in a brush with the rich and famous. Jobs's authenticity wins him points.

Why do people so often feel a little let down after the big moment of meeting an executive? Here are a few reasons:

- Our expectations of what the encounter will be like can be unrealistically high. The main goal is to have a positive encounter so that you will perhaps have positive name recognition in the future. If you walk away with your career unscathed, mission accomplished. You really can't expect to accomplish much in these brief encounters. This is not *Wedding Crashers* or *Pretty Woman*; it's just another a corporate function.

- Our expectations of the interpersonal skills of the executive may be too high. Some executives are not highly responsive and may not give you the immediate recognition, attaboy, or warmth you had hoped they would. The Steve Jobs story illustrates this.

- We never know what is going on in the mind of the executive. You may have made a better impression than you think.

You may be more successful than you realize

It is not uncommon to find out through the grapevine, sometimes years later, that a person made a better impression than he or she thought. Consider the full value of what transpired in the encounter. Have you tallied up all of your takeaways? If you learned something about the executive or the business or the company, count it a success. If the executive learned anything about you, call it a slam dunk!

MEETING AN EXEC OR KEY BUSINESS CONTACT THROUGH A FORMAL INTRODUCTION

Office etiquette is based on courtesy and thoughtfulness, and at the core of this social code is *kindness*. What is the kindest way you can respond to someone in a social situation? Etiquette is also based on being presented at court to the king or queen of England, so the old-style rules dictated waiting to be recognized by someone of much higher authority. The rules are always in transition; still, I would wait a moment for an executive many levels above me to extend her hand to shake mine. I wouldn't, however, wait on someone at my level or the level just above. It depends on the culture. If I were at Google, I would extend my hand to any executive. If I were at a traditional company like IBM or a midsize hometown tax firm, I would observe the hierarchy.

So there are gray areas. In social etiquette, a man waits for a woman to extend her hand first to shake hands, but in business etiquette we do not differentiate between genders; that is considered a form of bias. Still, if you are in a business setting, you may find some women who prefer not to shake hands. Women may find that some older white males do not feel comfortable shaking their hands. And more and more we are finding people who have stopped shaking hands because of cold and flu viruses passed in this manner. If you meet someone who is hesitant to take your hand, then graciously move back and give the person an out. If you see an unfamiliar executive who is many levels above you but is smiling at you and trying to engage you in conversation, you might extend your hand. By traditional rules, if an executive is many levels above you, then wait until he or she extends a hand first. But if you are reading the executive's face and see a willingness to meet you and engage you, that's a moment to step forward and show some initiative by extending your hand.

In a job interview, you should always extend your hand, even if the interviewer is several levels above you. A handshake is customary in this situation. Be sure if you shake hands with one person in a panel interview that you shake hands with everyone, regardless of gender or status. But don't extend your hand if the other person is trying to drink from a cup or is holding items that will make a handshake awkward.

INTRODUCTIONS: WHO'S ON FIRST?

One of the most confusing parts of business etiquette is the business introduction. The rules have changed from the day that men, like loyal subjects, were always presented to women, even if the woman's status was lower in the organization. Also, businessmen and women are all expected to shake hands today. *Etiquette International* gives an overview of the new rules:

> *In business, introductions are based on power and hierarchy. Simply, persons of lesser authority are introduced to persons of greater authority. Gender plays no role in business etiquette; nor does it affect the order of introductions.*
>
> *For example, you would say, "Mr./Ms. Greater Authority, I would like to introduce Mr./Ms. Lesser Authority." However, the person holding the highest rank may not be Mr./Ms. Greater Authority. A client, for instance, always takes precedence over anyone in your organization, as does an elected official.*

("Introductions," Etiquette International. www.etiquette international.com/Articles/Introductions.aspx)

STEPS IN A FORMAL INTRODUCTION

The following is a summary of how that first moment should go as you are introduced to an executive.

- Shake hands and sustain eye contact.
- Say that it is a pleasure to meet the executive or that you have looked forward to meeting the executive,

but don't gush. If you are part of a host department or committee, welcome the executive.

- If you have a friend, interest, or project in common, mention it in fifteen words or less.
- Disengage if the executive needs to move on. Tenacity in this situation can backfire.

If the executive gives you the opportunity to pursue the conversation beyond the introduction, then use all the strategies earlier in this chapter to ensure that your conversation will leave a positive impression of you as a credible professional.

A LASTING IMPRESSION

In summary, how you meet and communicate with people is probably the single greatest determinant of how successful your career trajectory will be. Being effective in meeting executives is especially valuable for a successful future. Make sure that you leave a memorable impression of your professionalism, high energy level, and intelligence.

In many relationships, people later discuss the moment of first meeting and how that led to a lasting friendship. Often, college friends who remain close for life will recall that first moment of meeting; married couples do so as well. Just as important are the moments of meeting people who could be long-term members of your career network or who could refer you to someone who hires you into the company where you will build an amazing career.

You never know when a moment may require your best communication style, so the wisest thing is to try to treat every first meeting as if it could be very important to your career. Present yourself to each person you meet as a highly professional, thoughtful, and knowledgeable individual. The person you are meeting today may be your partner on a project one day or may be your customer five years from now.

Whether you are a nurse who delivers opinions on insurance cases from your one-person office in your home office or an executive director for a large governmental agency, building relationships will always be an important factor in your success. You must build relationships with those you report to, sell to, buy from, and manage. Make the foundation of that relationship-building—the first moment of each encounter—a strong and positive experience. Take this chapter's recommendations and prepare yourself to wow the people you meet in the workplace and beyond.

2

THE **FIRST MOMENT YOU MEET** THE **INTERVIEWER** FOR **YOUR NEXT JOB**

I magine it's the day of your big interview for THE job—the job you know is perfect for you. You have dressed for success; you have researched the company; you are completely prepared for this interview—or are you? It may alarm you to hear this, but the first few seconds of an interview are powerfully influential, and first impressions do count. You may be well versed in the history and products of a company, but if the interviewer sizes you up and is unimpressed by his first moments with you, he may not be open to hearing what you have to offer. Interviewers judge you by whether they feel a connection—that mysterious thing defined by some people as chemistry, others as rapport, still others as synergy. Whatever it is, it has little to do with what is on your résumé. Strangely enough, what happens in those first moments of an interview is disconcertingly similar to falling in love.

If this sounds sketchy to you, just think of a past interview you went on in which you knew your skills, experience, and education were perfect for the job. It was as if your career fairy had reached down and custom designed a job just for you, then led you to the interview. Yet someone else got the job. How did that happen? It could be that the interviewer met another applicant, got all starry-eyed, and viewed that individual as the dream candidate. How can you get interviewers to fall in love with *you* as a candidate? Here are some principles to follow for making the fireworks happen when you meet the interviewer for the job of your dreams.

YOU ARE HOW YOU LOOK

When you walk in the door, you want it to be love at first sight. You want the interviewer to think "Now *that's* what I'm talking about!" How do you dazzle the interviewer by looking the part she is trying to fill? Here are some easy steps:

- Dress like your boss-to-be. Your image should be close to the image that the person you will be reporting to already has. If you are interviewing with a Big Eight firm, you may have to go out and invest in a more expensive suit, a more conservative shirt or blouse, or a more subdued, thicker silk tie or scarf. You may also need to do some research. Google your boss-to-be and see if there are any photos online. The image you see may inspire you to opt for a less-youthful-looking hairstyle or to wear less jewelry. Managers like to hire people they feel will fit right in. Although most managers do develop their employees, they don't go out looking for projects to take on. Try to emulate (but not slavishly copy) the style and dress of the boss and the most successful top reports on the team you hope to join. If you know someone in the company, ask what the preferred look is.

- Get plenty of sleep the night before, and don't drink. If a candidate comes in the morning after an evening out involving drinks with friends, the alcohol may still be exuding from his pores. His eyes may look tired or bored, and his energy level could be marginally lower. Managers hire people who have the energy to come in and start working hard immediately. If you come in visibly needing sleep, the interviewer may think your credentials are great but have serious doubts about your capacity for getting things done. You want people to think VA-VA-VOOM! not *ho-hum*.

  Another reason to get at least eight hours of sleep the night before is that sleep is the most powerful secret weapon for answering tricky interview questions. Even if you have read every interview book on Amazon, you can never completely anticipate the questions an interviewer will ask. When your mind is rested, your memory and response time are better. All those brain synapses will be clicking away and making dynamic connections so you can come up with brilliant answers to those unexpected questions. Come in looking bright and rested and feeling good.

BEFORE YOU STEP INTO THE INTERVIEW: LAST-MINUTE TIPS FOR RELIEVING STRESS

The minutes before you walk through the door and introduce yourself to the receptionist are critical. The following last-minute pointers will increase your chances of landing the job.

Be sure you have plenty of blood flow to your brain. Blood carries oxygen, vital for thinking up those great answers to challenging questions. You may be really smart, but if you are breathing nervously and shallowly, you may suffer from minor oxygen deprivation and not be your sharpest. How do you increase oxygen? About five minutes before you walk in the door of the interview, oxygenate your blood with this deep breathing exercise:

1. In a comfortable seated position (this is important), forcefully breathe out through your mouth. Pretend you are blowing out fifty candles on a birthday cake. Keep blowing until the last imaginary candle is out and all the air is out of your lungs.
2. Now breathe in through your nose, as deeply as possible. Fill your lungs completely full.
3. Repeat these two steps s-l-o-w-l-y five to ten times. Don't do this too fast or you could pass out.

You can do this exercise in the car before you enter the office for your interview. And throughout the interview, don't forget to breathe! Relieve tension by doing this muscle relaxation exercise:

1. Be seated. Start by arching your feet. Contract the arch of each foot, as if you are trying to grip something between the ball of your foot and your heel, squeezing as hard as you can. Hold the squeeze for ten full seconds. Count the seconds by saying, "One-Mississippi, Two-Mississippi, Three-Mississippi," and so on. Then release and relax.
2. Next, tighten the muscles in your calves as hard as you can. Hold for ten seconds. Release and relax.
3. Proceed in sequence from your toes to your head, tightening and releasing your thighs, buttocks, stomach muscles, shoulders, neck, and forehead. Then tighten your fingers, palms, and upper arms, holding each for ten seconds before releasing.

At the end of the exercise, your muscles should be more relaxed and oxygen should be reaching your muscles and brain more efficiently. Use these strategies for relaxation and breathing whether you are communicating with one person or a group. You can use these techniques discreetly, while sitting in a reception area or in a car just before embarking on an important conversation. Being short of breath is a common problem for anxious job applicants when first meeting an important contact, and these remedies offer dramatic relief. Learn and practice these and other techniques for preventing breathlessness, shakiness, and slumping; practice them even when you don't have an interview. When the time comes for that all-important interview, you will be ready. With a little bit of preparation, you can learn to project the kind of energy and initiative that hiring managers want on their teams.

LOVE AT FIRST SIGHT

Like most infatuations, having the interviewer fall in love with you begins with a smile. Many facial expressions can be misunderstood, but the smile always makes a good first impression. A look of apprehension about the interview can be mistaken for evasiveness or hostility; a face that shows fierce concentration can be misread as expressing anger issues or confusion; and an amused look can be read as sarcasm or sneering. The only antidote to all these ambiguous looks is the unambiguous smile—open, appealing, warm, and direct.

A person can fall in love with someone just because he is so flattered that the other person is crazy about him. Simply put, we like people who like us. Interviewers are no different. So smile right before you go into the interview, and then smile at the interviewer when you meet. It is disarming and gets the meeting off to a positive start.

If you first appear with a smile on your face, you will be a more attractive candidate. Also, work up your excitement for the job. One well-qualified candidate we know recently lost a job to someone less qualified. She went back to each member of the interview panel to ask for advice for future interviews. All agreed that she had not seemed enthused or passionate about the new job. It had been clear that the other candidate had really wanted the job.

Also, practice your Mona Lisa smile. Some job candidates frown or look worried when they are actually just listening very intently to the interview questions. Remember that your face is never in neutral; it's sending a message even when you are not the one talking. What is your face communicating to the interviewer as she speaks? A pleasant look on your face will convey goodwill. A forehead wrinkled in worry or tension can look unpleasant. Practice a pleasant listening expression, much like that of the Mona Lisa. This look isn't one of exuberant gaiety; it is pleasant, tranquil, and personable. Ask colleagues or friends for feedback on your "listening face." Avoid narrowed eyes and knit brows. Squinting can make you look shifty and distrustful. And don't be thrown off if your smile is not returned, though usually it will be. Some people are not used to being smiled at and may not respond in a way you can observe. That does not mean that you have not left a positive impression.

THE PERFECT HANDSHAKE

Offer the perfect handshake. How do you develop the perfect handshake? It has four parts: webs, grip, shake, and eye contact.

WEBS. The web of your hand is the loose skin that bridges the gap between your thumb and your index finger. When you shake hands, your web must touch the web of the interviewer. If webs don't touch, you have not engaged.

GRIP. The grip is just what it sounds like. It is how you squeeze or grip the interviewer's hand. The most mocked and talked-about loser handshake is the dead fish handshake, meaning that the grip is very weak. Male interviewers in particular seem to view this type of handshake as a red flag. The dead fish handshake can signal a lack of confidence, strength, or energy, none of which is good.

A close second as the kiss of death in a handshake is the bone-crusher, squeezing the interviewer's hand too hard. The bone-crushing handshake can actually anger the interviewer—never a good start. Bone-crushers can also be perceived as acts of one-upmanship. Overcoming your interviewer's grip is a competition you ultimately can't win. Even a handshake that grips just a bit too hard can be taken as a sign of neediness or poor judgment.

SHAKE. How many times should you shake a person's hand? Two or three times. Don't continue to shake as you talk. Just greet, shake a couple of times, and disengage. Any longer than that will make the interviewer uncomfortable. Any less shake may feel like holding hands, and we don't want that.

EYE CONTACT. The final and most important part of the handshake has nothing to do with the hands: it concerns your eyes. Making eye contact at the moment you shake hands is imperative.

How do you know whether yours is a winning or losing handshake? Ask! Try this experiment. Ask five of your friends to shake hands with you and give you feedback. Ask them to read this section describing webs, grip, shake, and eye contact. Then ask them to tell you if you need to improve in any one of those areas. If two people tell you that you are gripping too tight, then you know you need improvement. I recommend asking at least five people. You need to get a consensus. If you ask only your best friend, he or she may be a bone-crusher and not give very objective advice. More people equals more valid data.

WHAT TO SAY IN THOSE
CRITICAL FIRST MOMENTS

Now that you have entered the door and shaken hands, what do you say? The following are the basics:

- Greet the interviewer. Say "Good morning" or "Good afternoon," followed by the interviewer's name. People like to be greeted and acknowledged by name before you start hawking your résumé. Not sure how to pronounce the interviewer's name? Find out in advance! If the company is large, you can call a receptionist or administrative assistant to find out.

- Be interested in the other person. This is a golden rule with people we meet in other situations, and interviewers, believe it or not, are just regular humans too. They are susceptible to the human need to be liked and admired and to have their egos stroked. Your face and your responses should convey *subtly* but unmistakably that you find the interviewer fascinating. That notion of subtlety is critical, because fawning over an interviewer is a big no-no. So don't cross the line by overdoing your responses. Use good judgment and good taste.

The key to good conversation in an interview is to listen. Listen for anything the interviewer shares with you about himself, his job, his department, his health, his philosophy, his vacation—pretty much anything that is interesting to him. Do not be nosy and probing, but briefly respond to anything he says; don't just leave his remarks hanging there unacknowledged. Be cautious, though, about getting too personal.

Here are some examples of comments from an interviewer and possible responses:

COMMENT BY INTERVIEWER: "I apologize for the way I sound, but I have a cold."

POSSIBLE RESPONSE: "Colds and flu are everywhere these days." Or "Have you had it long?" Or (only if you know the interviewer flies a lot) "It's hard to avoid germs when you fly a lot."

COMMENT BY INTERVIEWER: "I am sorry we had to delay the interview, but I have been on vacation."

POSSIBLE RESPONSE: "Vacations can reenergize you, but I'll bet you're playing catch-up with emails and calls." Or "I hope it was a fun vacation and not one of those build-a-deck-on-your-house vacations so many people are taking."

COMMENT BY INTERVIEWER: "I want to interview you before my partner does because I have to leave at 4:30 for my daughter's softball game."

POSSIBLE RESPONSE: "Oh, I hope it's a good game. What position does she play?"

COMMENT BY INTERVIEWER: "Our department has been so overloaded lately and I have not gotten to these interviews as I should."

POSSIBLE RESPONSE: "Sounds like your group is pretty vital if you have lots of projects. Is the overload due to short staffing, or new business, or have you identified another reason?"

COMMENT BY INTERVIEWER: "I hope you didn't get into too much traffic; it took me over an hour to get here this morning."

POSSIBLE RESPONSE: "It wasn't bad; I came from the north," or "The new toll road really helps."

Keep the conversation positive and interested, but not invasive or personal.

WHAT NOT TO SAY

Are there topics that are off limits? Definitely. The rules have changed as people have become more security conscious. Don't ask her where she lives; she may think you are a stalker. Don't ask her the ages of her children; she might think you are a pedophile. Don't ask her if there are problems with the department; she may think you are negative. Don't give her health advice or try to fix her.

Conversely, keep your own personal life to yourself at this early stage of the interview. Don't tell about your vacation or children unless you are asked; allow the interviewer to control the conversation during the first moments. If she values being in control and you try to take control of the conversation too early, she will be annoyed that you are wasting time on your personal stories in the first critical moments. Later in the interview, she may open the door to such a non-work-related conversation, but the opening portion of the interview is too early to start talking as if you are friends.

How do you begin a meaningful conversation with the interviewer? By paying close attention to the interviewer's signals during the greeting, you can usually tell whether the interviewer wants to control the interview or if she wants you to do so. Most interviewers have an agenda in mind, even if it is not a written one. They have envisioned the general direction that they hope the conversation will take. Allow your interviewer to run with that, if possible. The interviewer will generally start the process for you by saying something like "Tell me something about yourself" or "Tell me about your career." Your responses can include a bit about your personal life, like where you are from or that you led the United Way campaign for your company last year. Still, the bulk of your answer should be about your career. Listen carefully so that you can be responsive to what the interviewer asks. If the interviewer asks about your career, do not include anything except your job history and accomplishments. Leave the hometown and volunteer work out entirely.

For any open-ended question about yourself, hit just the high points. If this is the first question, the interviewer wants an overview, not a detailed explanation of what you did at each position. You can include elements like these:

- **Summarize your responsibilities in each job.**
- **Add to this summary a comment about at least one thing you accomplished in that job.** Show a history of making a contribution to every job you've ever filled. Describe what you improved, streamlined, or made more cost-effective. Talk to the interviewer about savings in labor, materials, and time. Talk about your sales awards or other ways you brought profit or improvements to your workplace. When you are preparing for the interview, try to think of what you've done in a job that the person before you did not do. How did you leave a task or a department better in some way than when you found it?
- **As you talk about each position held, give a positive reason that you left.** "I finished my degree and went to work in the accounting department of Belks," or "After

three years as an associate, I was ready for a management position; Hanover Assisted Living offered me a great opportunity, so I took it." Show a continual upward climb in your career. Don't hide plateaus or setbacks, but don't feel it is your responsibility to bring those issues up. You will probably be asked about any gaps in your résumé, but don't belabor the bad times in this initial summary of your entire career. You may say something brief, like, "When the auto industry went through challenging times and I left Ford, I took some time to regroup. I rethought my direction and wound up going to work in an entirely different field: medical products. I found that many of the skills I had learned at Ford were equally helpful at Rotech." Again, be uniformly positive.

- **Be positive and M.I.S.S.I.O.N. oriented.** Tailor your remarks to the position. Glean experience you have that aligns with the job and mention that experience.

  Example: "As you may have guessed from my résumé, I have been looking forward to hearing about the organizational development changes being made here at Healthdyne. Most of my recent experience has been invested in organizational development metrics."

- **Create three billboard statements.** Have you ever noticed how effective billboards whet your appetite and pull you in with just one intriguing nugget about a product or company? Billboards don't try to convey detailed information. They plant a captivating thought in your mind so you want to learn more. Billboard statements in an interview do just the same. They throw out a short fact that gives the interviewer an image of you as a success story. Your brief billboard statement makes you a candidate that the company wants to know better, advancing you to the next round of interviews or possibly leading to your being hired on the spot.

Find ways to weave those statements into the conversation. Always be responsive and answer the question you are asked, but lead into your strengths. Some sample billboard statements follow:

- "While I was at Teleflora, I increased orders by 12 percent."
- "I was promoted three times in five years."
- "The just-in-time inventory system I designed saved the company $4,000 a year."

THAT INDEFINABLE ELEMENT

Some call it luck or serendipity. Bob Smith, president of Lockard Companies, quotes Proverbs 21:1: "The king's heart is in the hand of the Lord; he directs it like a watercourse wherever he pleases." Several times in his career Smith has been offered a position that might have been expected to go to someone more experienced, but the person interviewing Smith felt a connection or was prompted by something inexplicable to make him the offer instead.

Smith says that some managers are not seeking to hire the same kind of person they have always had in the position; they are hiring for potential. Managers also ask themselves questions about what the interviewee would be like to work with:

"Can I trust him? Will he be diligent? What can he help me accomplish in the future?"

If you are interviewing for a job and feel that everyone else seems more qualified, don't let that sap your confidence. Be optimistic. The company may be looking for a fresh set of eyes to look at their products or processes. Interview with great confidence. You would not have made it to the interview stage if you did not have a shot at taking the position. Companies don't waste their time that way.

PUTTING IT ALL TOGETHER

Although there are many parts to an interview, the first few minutes have proven to be the most influential in winning candidates a job. The greeting, handshake, responsiveness, and career overview just described will help you make an immediate positive impression, establishing you as confident, personable, and a great addition to the staff. Yes, your degrees and experience are important, but people want to choose a candidate they can talk to on Monday morning about their weekends and occasionally grab lunch with at the corner deli. Many teams become almost like families, and it is critical to show you're a person who can build fruitful relationships with your team members and integrate well. Practicing the approaches in this chapter will help you demonstrate just that. Your interview gives you only a few moments to show how well you can relate to others and to present yourself as a valuable addition to the team. The approaches already mentioned will help you purposefully demonstrate that you have the personal and professional attributes the interviewer is looking for.

DIFFERENT RESPONSES FOR DIFFERENT INTERVIEWERS

Hiring is an expensive and time-consuming process for most companies. When hires don't work out, that is an even more expensive problem. Companies have learned their lessons about how costly these mistakes are, and most have developed a system of checks and balances. Various people will interview you, and each will have a unique slant on what he feels is most important in the interview. You may face one or more of the following interviewers during the longer interviewing process often required in most companies: a HR person, a future manager, and/or a new teammate.

HR managers are more content oriented: do you fit the job description? Hiring managers want to see what skill and experience gaps you can fill and that you are manageable. They are very much focused on "What can you do for me on a daily basis? What is not being done with excellence now, and what can you do to improve that situation?" Peers are more interested in how well you will work with them and your skill set. They will be more sensitive to interpersonal problems like competitiveness, lack of teamwork, or failure to pull your own weight. As you interview with each stakeholder, the information you talk about may overlap, but the focus will be on the issues most personally important to the interviewer.

Your career will be a series of new beginnings that will last for several decades. Making each new beginning a fresh and positive experience for the people you meet and for yourself is an enjoyable and productive way to spend your time as you build your career. You will meet a wide array of people as you seek or start jobs, as you work alongside people or for them, and as you move through a series of positions. Becoming adept at the approaches in this chapter will empower you to leave strong first impressions of yourself as a professional and as a person. The positive encounters will energize you and the people you meet. This is not just a way to make the most out of new beginnings—it's also a winning career strategy.

3

THE **MOMENT YOU** ARE **OFFERED** A **JOB**

T he excitement of hearing an employer say "We would like to offer you this position" may cause temporary euphoria and make you throw all caution out the window. The moment you are offered a job, you are in a better position to ask for what you want than you will be again for a long time. The company has invested a lot of time and energy in selecting you, so they want their offer to be accepted. Don't jeopardize the offer by being demanding or aggressive, but if the offer falls short of your expectations, consider asking that the offer be enhanced in some way.

Be sure to look carefully at the written job offer and review all the benefits. You may automatically assume that you'll have prescription drug coverage or that you have two weeks' vacation as you did in your last job. But you can't assume anything. Read the fine print.

If you're dealing with a very small company, they may make you a verbal offer. A two-person enterprise may not want to take the time to put together a detailed contract. If you don't want to jeopardize the job offer by insisting on a contract, you may ask for the offer in an email. Regardless of the company or the job, the real predictor of how successfully you will handle the moment you are offered a job is in the weeks prior to the offer.

PREPARING FOR THE JOB OFFER

As soon as you decide to interview for a job, you should start your research. Some topics are no-no's for the first interview, yet you need to know about them as soon as possible. Here are just a few of the areas you should do your best to familiarize yourself with before the interview:

- **Salary.** What is the industry norm for this position? Is it lower in your region? Higher? Do you know anyone who works for this company? Industry norms can be way off base for certain companies and geographic areas, so try to locate someone who can tell you what his company normally pays for this position.
- **Other compensation.** Pay for performance, bonuses, commissions can make an otherwise ho-hum job offer very lucrative.
- **Pension, 401(k) plan, and stock options.** These investment vehicles also can make a job offer much more valuable.

- **Travel.** How much travel is expected? Is it overnight? By air, rail, or car? Your car or theirs? If your flight gets in at midnight on Tuesday, are you expected to be in the office at 8:30 A.M. on Wednesday? If possible, ask another employee—the employer may view such questions as a sign that you are not willing to work hard.

- **Vacation and other time off.** Would you accept a lower salary if a company offered you combined vacation/personal use days equal to six weeks of vacation compared with another company that offered only two weeks? If a company is famous for being a great place for parents and is generous about time off to take children to appointments and activities, would that make a difference? If quality-of-life issues are important to you, the lower salary may be worth it.

- **Start date.** Will this job start immediately or is it part of a long-term hiring effort? Is the company staffing up for an expansion that won't take place for several months? If you are not willing to wait on this job, you may not want to invest your time in interviewing.

Brian Drum created the following checklist for military professionals entering the job market, but these items apply to anyone receiving a job offer:

- Training programs or mentoring
- Educational reimbursement
- Career advancement opportunities
- Hours/work schedule
- Vacation time/holiday schedule/sick time or PTO (Paid Time Off)
- Office location/telecommuting options

- Cell phones, PDA, laptops
- Administrative support
- 401(k) eligibility
- Pension plan
- Bonus structure
- Stock options
- Profit sharing
- Health insurance coverage
- Dental insurance coverage
- Disability
- Competitive work clauses
- Business travel
- Childcare
- Club memberships
- Employee discounts
- Parking
- Car/allowance
- Termination clauses

(Brian Drum,"Don't Accept that Job Offer Yet." August 8, 2007. www.military
.com/opinion/0,15202,145310,00.html)

Although you don't want to grill the interviewer about every item in Drum's list, you should know the answers to most of these questions before you decide on a job offer. You can find the answers to many of these questions about your employment offer on the company website and in literature that human resources may give you. Other employees are also good sources of general information, though their offer may not be identical to your offer.

THE MOMENT THE OFFER IS MADE

You have sailed through your interview (maybe several), and you are the chosen candidate. The offer may be made in one of the following ways or in a combination.

Large or traditional companies often make offers in this way:

- In your interview with the hiring manager, he may tell you he wants to hire you, or he may telephone you a day or a week after the interview to tell you. Sad to say, some busy managers take several weeks to make this much-anticipated call, due to vacations, distractions, and the difficulty of getting all internal forces marshaled together to approve the offer.

- You may be told that the manager cannot make the offer but that all offers come through HR.

- Be prepared for the HR person to be rather serious during the offer process, as this is a negotiation for the company. The HR representative must be cautious throughout the offer process, no matter how much you are trusted and valued.

- Here are some options for responding when the offer is extended:
  - "Being a part of Chastain & Sons has been my goal from the beginning. Thank you for the opportunity. This offer looks very good. May I call you tomorrow after I've had time to read all the details?"
  - Or, "I have looked forward to receiving this offer. I would like to take it home and read it and formalize this as soon as possible."

- Or, "The offer seems to be everything we have agreed on. Do you mind if I take it home and take some time in private to read it?"
- Or, "This is exciting. I am assuming that I have a day or two to read through the contract. It looks really good."

The point is to be *very, very positive* about the offer without legally committing to accepting the company's terms before you read the contract. Jobs are a valuable commodity, and you don't want to sound casual, as in "I'll get back to you."

- In a process like this, it is probably expected that you will take a day or so to review the offer. However, you should respond to the offer as soon as possible. If it takes you only a few hours to review the contract and see that it meets your expectations, don't wait until the next day—call right away.

- On your acceptance, you will be scheduled to meet with an HR representative to sign even more papers (insurance, security, and so on) to begin to make you a part of the company. Your actual hiring may depend on a background check or some psychological testing, if these have not been done in the interview process.

The process is different when interviewing with a smaller company because it may have fewer formal procedures and may not even have an HR department. The hiring process at small to mid-size companies may differ from the elements just listed, for example:

- If you are being hired by the owner of the company, she may even hire you during the first interview, and the human resources department may have no role until they are signing you up for benefits. This fast track to employment is rare, but it happens. Be prepared and knowledgeable about the company and, if possible, the likely terms of an offer before you go in, just in case an offer is made that day.

- You may have an appointment with human resources and then unexpectedly be told you can meet with the owner or hiring manager the same day. Do not hesitate to take this opportunity.

What if you are given a verbal offer but nothing in writing?

- Ask the person hiring you to put the offer in an email to you. Just say, "I very much want this job. Would you do me a favor that would help me be clear on some things? To help me understand what you are offering and so I can discuss it with [my spouse, family, employment consultant], would you mind summarizing the elements of the offer in an email and sending it to me? I would really appreciate it." This is a reasonable request.
- A second way of asking for a written contract is to say something like "I hope you understand that I will need to get an offer in writing before I can relinquish the job I have. An email will be just fine." Most people understand the hesitancy about giving up a job until the new one is a sure thing.
- If you get any push back over asking for a written offer, you must choose to believe one of two things:
  - Is this small, informal company going to think you are inflexible or don't trust them because you insist on a written contract? Though rare,

this can happen, especially in mom-and-pop organizations. Although no attorney or human resources representative would ever allow for the possibility of accepting a job without a written offer, be aware that some people do business this way. In some cultures, a prospective employer will even be offended if you ask for a contract, as one's word or a handshake are to be respected and trusted more than the written word. If you are dealing with someone from another culture (even some less sophisticated U.S. cultures), you may need to take the gamble and just say yes. Weigh the benefit of gaining this great job against the risk that some of the lovely perks you don't have in writing before you take the job will never materialize once you're on the job.

— Is the company promising things they don't want to be legally bound to deliver? What is your sense of this company? What is their reputation in the industry? In your community? Among their former employees? Make a well-considered decision. Again, the preparation before the interview is critical if you find yourself in this situation.

THE FINAL, FINAL ACCEPTANCE OF THE JOB

Finally, the moment arrives. You have read the offer. All details have been worked out. You are satisfied with the contract offered you, and it is time to say yes. Be sure to make this a strong, relational moment for the person hiring you. This moment is one of the early building blocks in your relationship with the employer and the entire company.

The manager you will be working for has a lot invested in your hiring. Think of the hiring process from his viewpoint. Despite the fact he has interviewed you and checked your credentials, there is usually a momentary thought of "I hope we are doing the right thing here" when an offer is made. A bad hire can cost the manager a huge amount of time and negatively affect the department for the entire year. Hiring managers actually have more to lose in a bad hire than the employee does. As an employee, you can simply walk away. A hiring manager will be living with his mistake for months. And you can be sure this misjudgment will show up on his next performance evaluation. A business owner has even more money on the line.

FOUR-POINT VERBAL ACCEPTANCE

When you accept the offer, make the moment a strong reinforcement that the decision is an excellent one. Include the following in your acceptance:

1. Clearly say how happy, delighted, or honored you are to accept the position.
2. Express excitement or enthusiasm over a specific part of the job you are looking forward to. This should align with a task or skill that is most important to the employer. Example: "I can hardly wait to revamp the inventory system to FIFO." Use industry or company terms. Call departments what your new employer calls

them. If they use the term IT for information technology, don't say IS for information systems.

3. Express gratitude for the opportunity. Again, be specific. Example: "I am grateful for the time you spent in bringing me on board to be the lead analyst on the new technical analysis team. It is a perfect match between my background and the needs of the department."

4. If you have not already been told, ask what you can do next to facilitate the process of coming on board.

Even if the HR person receives your acceptance, don't ignore the relational part of your acceptance. You will need help and guidance from the HR person. Go through a modified version of the preceding acceptance. Just add a couple of very specific things the HR person did that you appreciate and express your thanks.

THANK-YOU NOTES AND LETTERS

Don't forget to mail a thank-you note or letter for every interview, whether you are hired or accept the job or not. Your professionalism is always on view. Failing to follow up with a mailed thank-you letter or note is considered highly unprofessional. An email is not acceptable. Keep it simple and be specific about what you learned about the interviewer's company.

4

THE **KEY MOMENTS** IN A **PERFORMANCE REVIEW**

(INCLUDING ASKING FOR A RAISE)

Whether you are an employee experiencing your own performance review or the manager conducting the performance review for an employee, this workplace event can be very stressful. Interestingly, the manager who is conducting the review usually experiences more apprehension and stress than the employee being reviewed. Your manager feels she has more to lose in performance reviews than you do. She must be effective in giving reviews to poor performers, to either improve their performance or lay the groundwork to terminate them. If their performance is not productive, it harms the manager's results, potentially damaging her career.

Simultaneously, the manager must appraise the performance of top-performing employees. If she does not handle these reviews correctly, she can actually discourage a great employee. At the same time, great employees need and usually want to learn and grow, so the manager must suggest areas for performance improvement and challenging goals. You have to worry only about your own performance and career. The manager has that to worry about plus the outcomes for herself, for the departmental results, and for the individuals she manages.

Because reviews should be taking place at least annually, and in some cultures semiannually or quarterly, being prepared to respond successfully and productively is a critical job skill. This chapter shares the best communication practices for both roles: the employee and the reviewer. If you are a savvy employee, the moment when you ask for a raise can be one of the most rewarding but is a real nail-biter, so we address that process specifically.

SUCCESSFULLY EXPERIENCING A PERFORMANCE REVIEW

The date and time of your performance review was set a week ago. You walk into the conference room not knowing what to expect. You sit down with your manager and feel that she is completely in control of what happens next; after all, she holds all the cards. WRONG!

Whether your performance review results in some positive advances in your career or some setbacks is largely influenced by how *you* handle the experience. Here are just a few of the ways you can negatively or positively impact the outcome of your performance review:

HOW TO ACHIEVE NEGATIVE OUTCOMES	HOW TO ACHIEVE POSITIVE RESULTS
Go into the review like a condemned person, and you could set in motion a self-fulfilling prophecy. Your boss can be affected by your own assessment of your own value. Don't signal low self-worth.	If you go into the review like an energetic, positive employee who is confident in her skills, you have a better shot at inspiring your boss's confidence in your abilities.
Go into the review with the attitude that it is the boss's meeting and that he is the only one who needs to prepare with the facts, questions, and objectives needed for a results-oriented meeting.	Collect as much concrete information about your accomplishments and performance as possible: time savings, efficiencies, sales, error reductions, and so on. Compile the information in a succinct presentation that allows you easy access to the information during the review. Use as many hard numbers as possible: percentages, dollar amounts, numbers of widgets. Along with convincing facts about your performance, you should also be prepared mentally. Establish a few goals for the meeting. Do you want to illustrate that the portfolio you manage outperformed the market by 5 percent even though the value of the portfolio is down for the year? Do you want to provide evidence of existing business you saved despite new sales being flat? Are you the marketing director of a local museum and want to share the creative ways you have increased visitors and visibility for your venue? As a convenience store manager, have you added products that have made the store more profitable?

CONTINUED >>>

HOW TO ACHIEVE NEGATIVE OUTCOMES	HOW TO ACHIEVE POSITIVE RESULTS
Assume your manager's preconceived notions are unchangeable.	See it as your role to provide insight into your performance by providing information your manager may not have. Sometimes a busy manager completely overlooks or forgets information critical to your evaluation. More than one employee has seen his manager amend a rating once all the information is shared in a concise and factual way.
Feel victimized that the manager wants more and more from you when you are already stretched thin.	Always be willing to say you will strive to reach goals set by your manager. Demonstrate excitement and commitment to being developed into a stronger contributor. Every employee can be improved.
See comments and evaluations as set in stone and unalterable.	Even if you can't see how it is possible to perform at a higher level than you do now, you can agree to at least part of a new goal. Ask whether you can be given resources or more time to reach the goal. Don't say that you can't reach the goal; ask for your manager's help to achieve the goal. Get him invested in your success.
When confronted with criticism about your performance, defend yourself vigorously and make it clear that your estimation of your performance is as valid as your manager's estimation.	Accept constructive criticism graciously and ask for advice on how you can improve. Entertain the idea that your boss has a different perspective and may see some things you don't see. The weaknesses your boss identifies may be the skills or traits barring you from your next promotion, so agree to try to improve.
If you feel you deserve a raise, don't mention it, but hope the interviewer will do the right thing.	If you feel you deserve a raise, ask for it politely and skillfully.

Going into the interview prepared will create an overall better impression of you as an employee. Simultaneously, being willing to accept constructive criticism will win more support from your manager than resistance or defensiveness.

STRATEGIES FOR A SUCCESSFUL REVIEW

Here are some other strategies for triumphing in a performance review instead of being a victim.

1. Ask "how" questions, not "why" questions. Ask your boss how you can improve in any area she has identified as a weakness. Ask this in a manner that expresses your sincere desire to improve, not in a manner that says to your boss, "Prove to me there is a way to improve, because I don't see it." Ask for suggestions and specific strategies.

2. Ask for incremental help from your boss. If you want to make sure your next review is better, ask your boss to give you feedback if he sees something going awry before the next performance review. If you can identify a problem and fix it, you may receive a better review next time. Also, you will learn more from just-in-time feedback than feedback that may come weeks or months later.

3. Thank your boss for identifying ways to make you better. Express verbally that you understand that constructive feedback is a method of improving your value to the department, your company, and yourself as a professional.

4. State your short-term and long-term goals for yourself and ask your boss what you need to do to achieve these goals. Begin to position yourself as a person who primarily wants to do this job well but that your secondary goal is to prepare yourself to advance in a long-term career with the company.

5. Ask for training or other developmental aid—this is a prime time to do so. Is there a course you can take to improve your performance or prepare yourself for the next position you may hold in the company? Ask for that training, coaching, or ways to gain other experience during the review.

6. Be sure to follow up the performance review with an observable behavior that demonstrates you are trying to act on the feedback you were given. For example, if your boss has criticized you for not making collaborative decisions with your staff, form a focus group the following week to help you make an upcoming decision. If you heard that you do not plan your time efficiently, mail your boss your improved Outlook schedule for the upcoming week or month. Don't wait passively, hoping your boss will notice you are taking steps to improve; share the evidence of your efforts. Bosses find this type of response to their advice gratifying and validating to them as managers.

7. If you believe you are due a raise, this is the time to discuss it. Using a thoughtful strategy, approach your boss in a polite and collaborative way. (This topic is covered more thoroughly later in this chapter.)

POSITIVE RESPONSES TO
PERFORMANCE REVIEWS

Saying out loud that you appreciate and plan to act on developmental feedback from a performance review can take many forms. The following are some ways to express that you are a valuable employee—and committed to becoming even more valuable:

- "You have given me some insights into my performance that I did not have. I am going to do everything I can to improve in the areas you pointed out."
- "I appreciate your candor about the areas where I need to improve. You can count on my commitment to improve in those areas."
- "What was really helpful to me in this performance review was not just your comments on my developmental areas but also your acknowledgment of areas in which I am on the right track or excelling. Thank you for taking the time to fully appreciate both sides of my performance."

Attorney Susan James gives her superiors at Regency Healthcare lots of credit for her performance development. She lets them know she welcomes the feedback, as they have entrusted her with a great deal of responsibility. The open flow of feedback between Susan and her superiors means they are generous with their affirmation of the good job she is doing and can mention changes they want to see before there is a problem. It works for everyone. Susan is a courageous and effective decision maker in a difficult industry, and part of her confidence stems from the fact she knows she is backed by her superiors.

Joe Ratway of Performance Advantage says that the employees he sees who seem to shine from the outset of their careers are the ones who make themselves vulnerable enough to ask superiors for feedback and then actually try to change their behaviors. He says that rather than spending one minute in defensiveness in response to difficult feedback, these courageous performers say to their superiors, "How would you counsel me? How would you coach me to change?"

ASKING FOR A RAISE

Asking for a raise can be nerve-wracking for many reasons. Although the goal is to improve their financial and career position, raise-seekers often fear they are running the risk of actually losing something. Some even fear that, just by asking, they risk losing their jobs at a later time. This rarely happens. Still, the fear of the unknown is all over this situation of approaching your boss for a raise. For that reason, and to overcome the awkwardness that attends even asking for money, you should prepare to do the asking in the right way. Asking for a raise is a three-stage process; follow it, and you will demonstrate you know what you are doing.

Stage One: Doing research and strategic planning
Stage Two: Delivering the request for a raise
Stage Three: Following up on the answer to your request

If you skip Stage One and go immediately to Stage Two, you greatly reduce your chances of getting this raise. If you skip Stage Three, you greatly reduce your chances of getting the *next* raise you ask for.

STAGE ONE: RESEARCH AND PLANNING

The most important factor in your getting a raise is the research and planning you do in Stage One. Before you even start, have a clear picture in your mind of exactly what you are asking for. What is your goal? Is it a dollar amount? A new commission structure? Also, do you have allies in the department who can support you in this? Do not go over your manager's head, but do ask for advice and support from colleagues, unless the situation is competitive and there are few dollars to give out.

Ten topics to research why you deserve a raise

Here are just a few of the questions you need to research prior to developing a strategy for asking for a raise:

TOPIC TO RESEARCH	APPLICATION TO STRATEGY
What are the industry norms for pay in your area?	If you are earning less than the industry norm, then you should include this fact in your presentation. Good sources are the Human Resources link at About.com, salary.com, salaryexpert.com, and payscale.com.
What are your colleagues making?	Your colleagues may be making more than you do because they asked or because they were hired away with a salary incentive from another firm. Check this out discreetly if you can.
Are salaries higher in your geographic area?	If you are a market analyst in New York and your colleague is a market analyst in Anniston, Alabama, then you will need a higher salary based on cost of living.

CONTINUED >>>

TOPIC TO RESEARCH	APPLICATION TO STRATEGY
Do you have a skill or ability that some of your colleagues don't have?	Do you know how to use software, equipment, or other resources that some others may not have mastered? Are you great technically in an area that the company relies on?
Do you fill a void? Is there something you do that everyone takes for granted?	If you are on a sales team and everyone always takes for granted that you will write the proposal, you are filling a highly valuable void. Include that service as part of your strategy.
Do you have years of experience your present company is not counting?	Did you have years as a co-op or intern that you can ask your boss to count as experience? Would she count your years in the same position or field in another company?
How many years has it been since you have had a significant raise?	You may think your boss shares your keen awareness of how long it's been, but you are probably wrong. It's OK to bring facts like this to your boss's attention in a businesslike (not whiny) way.
Have you taken on any additional responsibilities or duties or staff? Will you be asked to do so in the next year?	As companies do more with less, jobs are being combined at a savings to the company. If you are taking on these added duties, ask whether some of that savings can be passed on to you in the form of a raise.
Have you written an article, won an account, or done anything special to merit a reward in the form of a raise?	Sell your boss on the potential you have to make unique contributions. Ask to be rewarded for the added value you bring to the company and to be incented to continue doing so. Point out that creativity and innovation are touted to be the differentiators of successful companies in the next decade.

CONTINUED >>>

TOPIC TO RESEARCH	APPLICATION TO STRATEGY
Have you saved the company money or time in any way?	Compile all the numbers you can to support the way you have saved the company money on supplies, streamlined processes, or done anything else that saved time, money, or resources for your company. Don't forget that great relationships with vendors can save your company money.

Make it easy for your boss to give you a raise

Your boss has to justify giving you a raise. Companies are not eager to hand out money these days. As employees value the jobs they have, fewer of them are asking for raises. Managers must justify to *their* superiors why you should be given more money for doing the same job. Your research, compiled into a succinct, compelling presentation, will give your boss the ammunition to go to his superiors to get more money for you. If you do the hard work for him—giving him the solid reasons for rewarding you—then he is far more likely to overcome his hesitancy to begin the fight for more money for you. So research all these questions online, through word of mouth, through colleagues, in industry journals, and through search tools like EBSCO. If you cannot find the information, ask a business librarian at your local university to help you.

All of the reasons just enumerated can win you a raise. Researching them is your job, because every employee *wants* a raise, but you will be prepared to make a case that you *deserve* a raise.

STAGE TWO: DELIVERING THE REQUEST FOR A RAISE

In the past, you may have just taken a deep breath and blurted out a rather nervous or emotional request for a raise. You may even have sounded whiny. This is the moment to change all that. This time, you will be one professional talking to another professional about a good business decision. Here is how to proceed:

1. Follow all the advice in chapter 2 on how to prepare for an interview: get plenty of sleep, do relaxation exercises just before the interview, and so on.

2. Raises are usually discussed in the performance review. If this is the case, allow your manager to conduct the review first. She may already be planning to give you a raise, so allow her to do this her way. If she doesn't, you can always bring it up at the end of the review. If she says there is no time on that day, then ask, "May we schedule an appointment next week? This raise has become very important to me."

3. If the raise is not usually discussed in the review or if you have a reason to prefer to have this discussion at another time, be sure to make an appointment in advance with your manager. If your boss is not a morning person, be sure to schedule around this or other quirks.

4. Begin with a positive statement about what you have gained and learned over the past year, including your boss in the credit. Do not grovel or fawn, but do acknowledge his part in your development. Example: "Over the last year, our transition to a digital network has been challenging, but I am excited about all I've

learned and feel strongly I am a better professional now that I am proficient in digital networking. I want to thank you for assigning me to this project and for the training you brought in from our vendor. I also feel I am valuable in other ways; that's why I want to ask you to consider my reasons for asking for a raise."

5. State firmly that you would like to "discuss several reasons you deserve a raise at this time." Saying that your boss should "consider" the reasons makes it hard for him to give a no in this meeting. He may not have the authority to give you a raise, but he does have the authority to say he will consider your reasons. If he considers your reasons, he may share them with his boss, who may give the go-ahead. Also, saying that the raise should be considered "at this time" sounds as if there are reasons that are timely for you to be given this raise, and there are: your accomplishments.

6. At every point in this discussion, allow your boss to comment. Listen respectfully to his points.

7. The key moment in the request stage is when you present the written document listing your accomplishments, savings, and other reasons you have earned the raise. Having your reasons organized and printed out offers documentation and credibility. It sends the message to your boss that you are serious about pursuing a raise.

8. As you present the list, say, "I have summarized a few of the highlights of my performance that I believe merit a raise. With your permission, I would like to go over these with you." Again, you are getting incremental buy-in from your boss when you ask permission to go over your reasons.

BASIS FOR RAISE

1. Streamlined the invoicing process and cut the time to process by two minutes.	Two minutes per invoice x cost of time $0.75 (salary of each accounts payable processor prorated) x 4,000 invoices per year annually = $6,000 savings per year.
2. Eliminated one position on my team and assumed some of the duties; delegated others.	Estimated savings of $40,000 annually.
3. Changed vendors for supplies and increased discount from 15 to 20%.	Supply budget of $4,500 x 5% = $225.
4. Increased our internal ratings by our interdepartmental customers by 4% and reduced complaints by 8%.	Improved our performance feedback for every employee in the department, as these ratings affect our performance assessment.
5. Became proficient in editing JPEG and PDF files.	Improves efficiencies and quality of our reports; cuts the time we were losing by sending these to technical support.
6. Improved departmental morale by devising the Woody Award for the best performance in a given month, now awarded at the monthly staff meeting.	Employees are incented to perform at higher than average levels and are rewarded by acknowledgment, as performance pay has been eliminated.
7. Represented our company at the annual convention of TWWC, a major industry conference, bringing back ideas related to industry trends. I reported information at the September staff meeting.	Keeping current in the industry has value, and I brought that value back to the company through knowledge sharing.

9. Finally, ask for the raise. You must use a verb, because you want your boss to take action. Examples:
   - Based on these reasons and any observations of your own, would you support me by requesting a pay raise for me?
   - Based on my performance over the last year and given reasons such as the ones I have presented, will you consider giving me a raise?

   Be prepared to answer questions such as "How much did you have in mind?"

Bring the following aids to the performance review: your calendar, a typed sheet of your accomplishments and positive information about your performance (based on the research of the ten items above), as well as complimentary letters, emails or acknowledgments of your service from customers, executives, other departments, or vendors. Review the sample of a typed sheet of accomplishments (see opposite).

STAGE THREE: FOLLOWING UP ON THE ANSWER

You will need to be prepared for two possible outcomes: that the answer may be "yes" or the answer may be "no." Guidelines for successfully responding in either case follow.

What if the answer is yes?
Sometimes, your timing is perfect for asking for a raise, and the answer is a quick "yes" with even a comment that the raise was already in the works. You should be prepared to answer your manager if he asks you the amount of the raise you have

in mind. Ideally, you should ask your manager to suggest the amount. Often the manager will come up with a bigger number than the employee, so do all you can to encourage your manager to go first. Sometimes, however, your manager just won't, so be prepared with a number.

And don't forget to say thank you three ways:

- Thank your boss the moment she says yes.
- Send a written thank-you note to your boss.
- At a later time, say thank you again. When you are able to buy a car or move to a new place or place your child in a great preschool, mention the raise again. Many people love to play a part in their employees' prosperity—even though your raise was deserved. Allow people to participate in the good things that happen to you; they will become more invested in you.

What if the answer is no?

If your boss says no to a raise, always suggest an alternative:

- First and foremost, be polite and appreciative that your manager heard you out and considered you for this raise—no matter how you feel. Be professional. This is the person who can support you next time—or not.
- Always ask when you can be considered for the next raise and ask for steps you can take to earn that future raise. If at all possible, get these recommendations in writing, then start fulfilling everything on the list. If reviews won't take place again for six months, ask whether you might be considered in two or three months instead of having to wait the full six months. Your manager may have difficulty saying no twice.

- Ask if you can be rewarded in other ways: commission on certain items, incentive pay if you reach a really aggressive goal, or a PDA with paid service or laptop or company car.

WHAT IF YOU STRONGLY DISAGREE WITH YOUR PERFORMANCE REVIEW?

For whatever reasons, sometimes bosses just get things wrong. If in the performance review you are not able to present facts and statistics that prove you are worthy of a better evaluation, then consider the following tactics. Please note that these are risky. In most cases it is better to accept the review, demonstrate to your manager that you are striving to follow his leadership, and hope for a better review next time. In rare instances, you may feel that your boss has been unaware of some of your contributions or has been so incorrect about your performance review that it may actually harm your future with the company. Only if you feel strongly that the risk is worth it should you proceed to take steps following your performance review:

- Ask for some numerical goals you could strive for prior to the next review. For example, if your manager told you that you are not as productive in your accounts payable role as he would like, ask him the pace of invoice processing you should reach in order to improve your evaluation.
- Ask if your manager would mind including your one-page handout of your accomplishment in the folder

with his evaluation. (Be sure to bring that one-pager with you to the review just in case.)

- If you cannot convince your manager to amend your review, say that although you do not agree with the evaluation, you do respect him. Ask for more help in the weeks or months prior to the next review so that you can earn a better review next time.

EMOTIONAL RESPONSES TO REVIEWS: NOT A WINNING STRATEGY

No matter what happens in the review, do not become emotional. In fact, be sure to prepare yourself ahead of time for any kind of review and critique of your work. Employees are frequently caught off guard by inaccurate and unfair criticisms of their performance. But expressing anger, hurt, or shock is not a winning strategy for improving your next review. In contrast, handling unjustified criticism professionally can build your manager's respect and appreciation of you as a professional and lead to a better review next time.

How do you prepare for an unemotional and professional review? Much like interview preparation: get plenty of rest and be sure you have had a meal prior to the review. Don't let low blood sugar make you shaky or teary. Also, ask a friend to role-play the review with you. Give the friend some worst-case scenarios. Ask him to criticize you unfairly and then assess your response. Just talking this out will help you think through some better answers than you might otherwise have come up with.

A RISKY APPROACH THAT PAID OFF

The following story falls into the "don't try this at home" category, but there are some good takeaways.

Randy Lyle had a successful career with Georgia-Pacific, rising to director of logistics in the monolithic and complex company, but he got off to a slow start. Randy says, "For the first ten years of my career, I worked harder than anyone, hoping that someone would discover what a shining star I was and reward me, but that did not happen." Randy's goal was to be a branch manager, but he was ignored as he quietly waited for his various managers through the years to give him the position.

After watching some Tony Robbins tapes (I kid you not), Randy decided to take his career into his own hands. He went to his vice president—whom we will call Ted Caldwell—and boldly stated that he wanted to be a branch manager. The vice president said, "Randy, you would have to pass the very difficult management test we give for employees who want to go into those positions."

Randy said, "How do I sign up for the test?"

Caldwell dismissively said, "I will get you signed up for it through Neda, my secretary. She will call you."

So Randy waited. And waited. After a few months, it became obvious that the VP had no intentions of scheduling the test.

Randy was undeterred. He picked up the phone, called Neda, and said, "Mr. Caldwell said I was supposed to be scheduled for the branch manager's test. When is it?"

Randy had used his VP's name, so Neda got out the roster and got him scheduled right away. Randy passed the test with flying colors, became one of the most successful branch managers in the company, and eventually was chosen to be the president of one of the subsidiaries.

Being this aggressive is not usually recommended; on the other hand, being too passive is a surefire path to a dead-end career. Being intentional and assertive about asking for what you need and following up to make sure you get it are great strategies if you want to boost your chances of advancing at a faster-than-average rate of speed.

For most cases, Randy offers this advice: don't ask for a raise; ask for a promotion. Management is much more likely to respond positively if you ask for more responsibility than if you just ask for more money. Eventually, though not always at first, the money will follow.

Also, don't be afraid to ask your manager, "What do I need to do to get to the next level?" This question is especially important if you are turned down for a raise or promotion. Also, follow the same steps as if you were given a disappointing performance review, covered in the next section.

YOU'RE THE MANAGER: HOW TO CONDUCT A WINNING PERFORMANCE REVIEW

As a manager, you have many reasons to conduct a well-planned and well-executed performance review that leads to a positive outcome for the employee, the department, and you.

A successful performance review can accomplish several important goals:

- Improve the output and quality of the employee's work
- Help you meet or exceed departmental goals
- Enhance the morale and atmosphere of the entire department
- Aid in developing the employee to take on more responsibilities and new roles—developing talent from within is a highly cost-effective hiring strategy.

Communicate sooner rather than later

Perhaps the best advice about performance feedback is to give it as soon as possible. If an employee's performance is below acceptable standards, you owe it to the employee to help him correct it as soon as possible; most employees want this opportunity. If you don't, the behavior can become a comfortable habit and more difficult to correct.

Many managers have the habit of procrastinating when the feedback they have to offer may be uncomfortable. Delaying means the situation will only grow increasingly uncomfortable. As Bob Smith, president of Lockard Companies, says, "Bad news does not grow better with time."

Before the review

Preparation is key to a successful performance review, for managers as well as employees. Take the extra time to do a review right, and you can avoid the serious consequences of getting it wrong. You will emerge from the review with better results if you take these steps:

- Gather far more information than you think you'll need. Remember that the employee knows much more than you do about what she's been doing each day in her role. You should be as prepared as possible with statistics, examples, numbers of any kind, and concrete (not subjective) observations.

- Keep records, as they occur, of complaints, compliments, absences, or anything else that will be part of each employee's performance review. Do not trust your memory. Even if your memory is great, without documentation your observations are just he-said-she-said.

- Do not rush the review. Plan your day around it. Ideally, you won't do two reviews on the same day, and certainly never three. Allow far more time for the review than you think it will take. Great reviews are collaborations. If you want buy-in from an employee, you must be willing to hear what he has to say. You may be able to time your remarks to an hour, but you have no idea how long the employee's remarks will take. Allow for the possibility of a spontaneous and valuable discussion.

- Be sensitive to the employee's feelings and plan your wording in advance for areas of constructive criticism. Even the most mature employee can feel embarrassed or even hurt when her weaknesses are discussed. Choosing the right words can minimize the sting. For example, tell an employee that she can improve her communication with colleagues if she focuses on three or four main points instead of including so many details. This constructive advice is both kinder and more effective than saying that she talks too much. Focus on the positive outcomes of changing behavior; don't dwell on the negative.

- Role-play with a nonwork friend or coach to improve your ability to think on your feet in the interview. Remember not to mention names or other confidential information in the role-play.

Ten points for success: A performance review model

1. Open with a gracious statement of appreciation for the employee's experience, expertise in an area, or other point of value. Every employee brings something of value to the company. Note specifically something the employee brings to the table. For example, even an employee who has been slacking off could be greeted with, "John, it is always valuable to me to sit down with you in these annual reviews. You have more years of experience in Quality Assurance than anyone on the team, and I am always interested in your perspective on things."

2. Ask the employee if he has some things he especially wants to talk about today or any comments he has about his performance. Many employees will actually do the

manager's reviewing job for him if this important step is taken. Ideally, the employee will bring up any job gaps or weaknesses. It is always better for the employee to identify and own the need for improvement than for the manager to do so. Studies have shown that an employee is much more likely to improve performance if he brings up the developmental weakness than if his boss does. If the employee identifies the primary developmental needs, then skip to step four.

3. If the employee does not offer any constructive criticism of his performance, share with the employee the following agenda and ask again whether he wants to add anything to it:
    - Identification of developmental strengths
    - Identification of opportunities to develop further
    - Brainstorming strategies for professional development
    - Agreement on six-month development goals and strategies for achieving goals
    - Optional: Although we don't recommend it, many organizations give a rating at this point. Sometimes these ratings influence pay or bonuses. Usually these ratings should be discussed in a meeting separate from the performance review.

4. Begin by describing any accomplishments or anything praiseworthy the employee has done. End by noting particularly any areas that have improved since the last performance review.

5. Then say, "And that brings us to the areas for further development, so you can continue to increase your value as an employee and strong contributor to our team. What two areas would you say you would like to develop over the next six months?" This is your second attempt to get the employee to pinpoint and own his developmental weaknesses. If he does not, ask him, "Is there anything you would have done differently over the last six months?"

6. Whether the employee contributes or not, the next step is to add your observations and suggestions for improving the employee's performance. As you comment, allow the employee to discuss and offer new information.

7. Listen. It is critical that you listen and be willing to amend your opinion based on the employee's comments. Give the employee as much time as he wants to offer his thoughts. If the employee wholeheartedly accepts your original comments, Steps 8 and 9 will not be needed. Then state any possible rewards.

8. Amend your original assessment and goals if necessary and rewrite the new assessment and goals with the employee sitting there. After you have rewritten your comments, ask for the employee's approval or collaboration.

9. After you have negotiated for awhile, ask the employee, "Are you more comfortable with this amended assessment and goals than you were with the original?"

Note: If an employee's performance has been unsatisfactory and she is a candidate for possible termination, be sure to discuss the possible consequences of her behavior, including termination if the behaviors are not changed. Again, a discussion like this is only for employees who have not seemed willing to perform to necessary standards; it is a last resort after much developmental intervention by the manager.

10. End on a positive note. If you have any information about rewards for the employee, state it at this time. If there will be a resulting bonus or promotion, state it. If you have ideas for his long-term development, further training, or an improvement in his work conditions, this is also the time to announce it. Thank him for something specific he has contributed and suggest a follow-up conversation prior to the next formal review. If you feel he needs assurances about his job security or value to the team, be sure to offer that, if appropriate.

DEVELOP EMPLOYEES INSTEAD OF PUNISHING THEM

You will not always inherit a team of strong performers; in most cases, you will need to develop employees into strong performers. Your reputation as a manager will be built on how well you achieve goals through the people you manage, and developing them is the way to get greater performance from each one. Look for ways to coach them yourself, send them to training courses for their technical and professional improvement, and team them with their peers to cross-train in areas of strengths and weaknesses. Letting your employees know you are deeply invested in their short-term and long-term career success is not just a kindness; it is the smartest strategy to increase individual performance. The performance review is the event that offers the greatest potential to build employees' performance and improve your team's ability to meet the goals handed to you by the company.

As in any communication moment you will encounter in your career, performance reviews require preparation, thoughtfulness, consideration of what the other person has at stake, and the intent to improve the workplace for others and yourself. These same qualities and intentions can guide you through other communication moments that, like the performance review, are part conversation and part negotiation. It really is possible for communication moments like these to be win-win-win: winning for the employee, the manager, and the company that will ultimately benefit. Great communication will not only enhance your paycheck but also build relationships that can support your career on many levels. That value cannot be overestimated; it is worth the investment in handling the performance review—and every communication moment—with sensitivity and intelligence.

5

THE **MOMENT YOU MEET** YOUR **NEW TEAM**

The way you first meet a team or any group of people has a lot to do with the chemistry you will have with them and the role you will play for the rest of the time you are with this group. This is true whether you are meeting a team you are about to manage or are meeting colleagues on a task force or committee, or in your department for the first time. Why? Because the people you are about to meet could be the allies who will refer opportunities to you for the next twenty years. One of them could become your best friend and someone with whom you'll share career moments—both great and not-so-great. Another could leave the following year, go to a better company, and call and offer you a job at a higher level. On the other hand, if you don't handle the first impression well, one person could easily become an obstacle to your succeeding in reaching the team's goal. Another could just make your life miserable by second-guessing you because he does not feel confident about you. And still worse, one day a team member may be promoted to a higher position of a department where you want to work and his view of you as less than impressive could lose you a coveted position. Anything can happen—good or bad. Be sure to make the outcome a good one for yourself and all concerned.

MEETING YOUR NEW TEAM OF EMPLOYEES

Initially, we will explore the process of successfully taking charge of a team of employees soon after you are hired. Whether you are a team leader or executive, the approach to successfully meeting your subordinates and launching your initiatives follows much the same simple format. Employees at all levels have fears and insecurities about the new boss, they all have a need to be recognized for their abilities and experience, and they all want to be acknowledged personally as unique human beings who will be in a day-to-day relationship with you. Some people even look at their department or team as their "work family," as there are often many similarities to the family unit.

For one thing, any time there is a departure from the family or an addition, emotions run high and there is a period of chaos as the transition is made. During the transition roles are not well defined and communication processes must be felt out carefully. That first moment of your introduction into the group is critical to assuring employees that your relationship to them is constructive and positive and that they should not feel threatened. When your teammates meet you, they should say to themselves, "This new person seems sharp; she or he will fit right in and be enjoyable to work with."

Your task is especially difficult when the last manager was greatly admired or even loved. Even if the last manager did not perform well, he will have his fans. And some employees are going to complain about any manager, no matter how well the manager performs. These whining employees may have complained for years about the last manager, yet will be the first to say, "Well, our last manager didn't do it that way. Here's the way we have always done it."

It's also tricky to manage people who are more experienced in the subject matter of your department than you are. Grace Freedson tells of the time in her career at Barron's Educational Series when she moved from being manager of public relations to senior editor. She knew all about PR, but next to nothing about the editorial process. She did, however, know how to communicate with and manage people.

She asked lots of questions, in a style that said, "I'm interested" rather than a style that made her seem powerless and ignorant. More important, she listened to her people. Thanks to these approaches, she became a successful editor.

Happily, most employees are open-minded and will even be both excited to meet you and hopeful that all changes will be ones they have been wanting for a long time.

Some simple steps can make those first moments with your team a success. As is true for a military leader taking charge of the troops, a little advance planning and a definite strategy to capture their support and respect can yield spectacular results.

STEPS TO WIN THE SUPPORT AND ADMIRATION OF A NEW TEAM

Taking charge of a new team is a big deal for you and for them. It can also be a lot of fun. Fresh starts are often a time when employees put forth an extra level of effort to impress the new boss. Take advantage of that wave of enthusiasm and ride it to achieve some fantastic results in your first few months.

The process that follows has worked for many successful managers.

- **Go to key members in advance.** Develop allies and support. At this time, just build relationships and ask for their help. Don't set policy. Say you only want to get to know the person you are visiting.

  Training consultant Bill Robb says to "ask for their views upfront":

  "Before the meeting I'd send out a short note saying that I'm looking forward to working with them and a short biography. Then say 'Please send me five things we need to do as a team to be even more successful and serve our internal clients better.'

  "I've found that the best way to get buy-in and respect is by listening, listening, and listening. They'll love you!"

- **Acknowledge the skill, experience, and knowledge of individuals.** Know as much as possible before going into the group. Know what makes them unique. Know what value each employee feels he brings to the department. Prepare to be appreciative and acknowledge these specific gifts. Microsoft Online offers articles preparing team managers to be successful as they implement

software such as InfoPath and Excel. In an article enti-
tled "Getting Started as a New Manager," the following advice is offered:

First and foremost, as a team manager, you are the
supreme communicator. That, however, doesn't just mean
that you filter and route project information through the
correct channels—it also means building community and
a culture within your team that works around interper-
sonal problems and brings out the best in individuals. As a
team manager, you're also your team's liaison to the bigger
picture. That is, it's your responsibility to set goals for your
team that align with your company's objectives and to help
your team successfully reach those goals. Finally, you're the
monitor of your team's progress and overall skill set. It's
your job to evaluate individual team members' perfor-
mance, to facilitate the development and application of
their skills, and to hire new team members who comple-
ment and expand the overall team skill set as necessary.

("Getting Started as a New Manager," 2003, http://office.microsoft.com/
en-us/infopath/HA012192331033.aspx)

- **State your openness.** Demonstrate in a concrete way
  that you are open to the ideas of others. Say things such
  as one of the following:
    - "I will spend the next three weeks just learning
      from you."
    - "I cannot offer any guarantees at this point as
      I am still learning. But I can guarantee I will
      listen to everyone's ideas. If we can incorporate
      them to make the department better, then of
      course I will implement them."

- "I am looking for good ideas. I want to hear yours. I am open to your suggestions for making our department more profitable and efficient."
- "Our goal is to provide better service for our internal clients in marketing. I am ready to listen to any constructive suggestions for improving our department in pursuit of that goal."

- **Express a desire to learn.** Every business or department believes its identity is unique. You may experience some resistance from longtime employees who think that you can't possibly understand what it is like to do their jobs in this particular company and in this economy. Tell your new employees that you expect to be taught many things by them during your learning curve. Ask for any information that they can offer about their unique part of the department. Ask for constructive and specific information so that you can learn faster.

- **Start with the good news.** Ideally, you have been hired to make some things happen that will be welcomed. Say so in the first meeting. State anything that is sure to be received positively. It's usually best to save controversial ideas for your second meeting or for individual conversations. The first encounter with your team should be filled with good news.

- **Have something to say.** Although you want to be open, be prepared to offer some leadership. Acknowledge some of the goals your department has been charged with, and leave the door open to further collaboration. Tell the team you will be working with them to refine goals and establish some specific short-term objectives.

Share any industry knowledge you have that relates to those goals.

- **Don't set precedents.** For example, if your first meeting is on a Friday afternoon, don't dismiss everyone early in celebration of your arrival. Your staff may expect this perk every time.

- **End with a statement of appreciation and commitment to collaboration.** Be optimistic about the future and express full faith in the group. Say, "Thank you for making me feel welcome and for your expressions of support. I am fortunate that I am starting this job with a skilled and experienced team. Together we can collaborate to make each other and the department extraordinarily successful."

TEMPORARY POSITIONS CAN PRODUCE PERMANENT RESULTS

Just because you think you are in a temporary position or are working with someone on an interim basis, don't underestimate the importance of the impression you make. One of my favorite success stories is that of Robert L. Smith, Jr., president of Lockard Companies in Cedar Falls, Iowa. Bob is a much-admired leader in the business community and in the community at large. He did not start out as a success, however. In fact, at first he could not even get a job that used his college degree.

When traditional avenues for landing that first job out of college failed, he came up with an ingenious plan. Although none of the preferred employers was hiring, all were using temps for special projects. Smith decided to go to work for a temp agency used by a couple of his preferred employers—John Deere and a number of banks. He made up his mind he'd be the most amazing temp John Deere had ever hired.

There were challenges. The woman he reported to on his first day handed him some software he was totally unfamiliar with and just walked away. But Smith figured it out, and his performance was impressive—so impressive that a position was created just for him. Later, Bob landed a job with his first choice employer, a large bank. His work in the marketing department of the bank led to his eventually landing the credit analyst's position, which then led to his original goal: a commercial lending position. His leadership was noticed by a mid-sized local company, and he was later asked to take over as president at Lockard Companies. Many employees look at the jobs they have now and think that high performance in a lowly position is not important. The majority of highly successful executives made an impression at every level, even the lowest.

SUCCESSFUL COMMITTEES AND FOCUS GROUPS

You may be asked to spend some time on a committee or focus group with employees outside your area. This is a great opportunity for networking and building your relationships with people you may serve or may want to work with in the future. Meeting them follows much the same process just described, except that these groups are designed to be temporary. A successful group meets for a short time and usually delivers a successful recommendation.

Dr. Robert Warner, cardiologist and member of the Board of Trustees for Wellstar Hospitals, has served on both medical and financial committees in the healthcare industry. He says there are three stages to a successful committee or other temporary group: "A good committee is problem-oriented. You unify because everyone has one thing in common: you all want to solve the problem. The three steps in a successful committee are to identify the problem, solve the problem, and effectuate the solution."

Warner says that many groups identify the problem and come up with a solution, but it takes real leadership to effectuate a solution. The final step is never taken by some organizations, making all the time spent on steps one and two worthless.

OVERCOMMUNICATE

Because people differ in their preferred mode of taking in communication, one marketing professional told me she overcommunicates with team members. She sends messages orally and written. She leaves no doubt that she has furnished the information each person needs in a style that each person prefers.

She also views herself as a value-added part of the team. She asks herself, "What is the unique value I can bring to this committee or team?" Then she makes sure she delivers the value. As you might expect, she is a well-liked and highly regarded member of her team. She has worked successfully in the same company for over two decades.

BUILDING RELATIONAL CAPITAL

While you are on committees and focus groups, make the most of your time to build relationships with people who could be your allies or even hiring managers in your future.

Get to know your fellow members, their jobs, their challenges, their interests. Express sincere interest in their work and their department. Most people love to talk about what they are working on, so be a good listener. You will build rapport that will help you with the project your committee is working on now, but you will also build a foundation with professionals who may be in a position to help you in the future.

FIRST IMPRESSIONS COUNT

Every person, group, or company you ever join gives you a clean slate—a wonderful opportunity to improve yourself over your past performance. Prepare yourself to be successful before meeting these people. Study their needs, preferences, and styles before blundering ahead, without any preparation, into a group. Some things your parents told you are true: you never have a second chance to make a first impression.

6

THE **MOMENT YOU** ARE **FIRED**

WE HOPE THIS ONE NEVER HAPPENS TO YOU—BUT SMART EMPLOYEES ARE READY FOR ANYTHING.

You actually gain some huge advantages when you are fired. If you can keep your wits about you and realize how liberating this can be—that it could actually be an opportunity to advance your career—then you may discover some benefits you would otherwise miss. In the moment, it's tough to see being fired as an opportunity—but that is exactly what you have to do to help yourself come out of the situation with as much support, income, and goodwill as possible to help you gain that next great position. So pause, take a breath, then read on to see what you can do to feel and *be* successful in a situation in which it's more tempting to feel like a complete failure. Remember that this is only one event in your career. Being terminated is likely to happen to everyone at some time over the course of a career. Consider what some people have said, twenty years after a firing, when looking back on their careers:

- "Being fired from that job was the best thing that ever happened to me."
- "I never would have looked at a different industry had I not been fired."
- "Ironically, the next big career opportunity came from a company where I had been fired. I talked to one of my former colleagues with whom I had a good relationship, and he thought of me for the position."
- "This is the second time I have worked for this company. The first time I worked at XYZ company, I left with the first wave of downsizings. When the industry picked up, they called me and offered me a better job."
- "When I was fired, I was shocked that it could happen to me, a top performer. I was focused on how unfair it was. Now I know that it will happen to nearly everyone in one form or another over a career. I also learned that it is not about me. It is a business decision about finance and the structure of the company."

All of these comments were made by people who are highly successful but were once fired. Each statement highlights one reason to make your exit from a company as professional as every other milestone of your career. With more career mobility these days, one of the best potential employers you will have in the next decade is the one that is letting you go today. Companies change, management regimes change, and you will change in what you want from a company in different seasons of your life. Be sure to leave on excellent terms so that, if the right time should come—for you and for them—to reunite, the people there will want you back. That said, there are very real, legitimate reasons why employees can be fired, apart from layoffs.

WHY BOTHER?

You may be saying, "I don't want to ever be in this position again. I can't imagine anything that would make me want to work for this company again, so why bother with a gracious exit?"

Here's why. As you grow in your career and amass accomplishments, you may eventually become the most attractive candidate for a management or executive position that may now be far above your pay grade. Going back one day as a leader and not an individual contributor can change your original perception of the company. Similarly, going back as an executive when you had previously been only a manager can give you an entirely different slant on a company—and the power to change what you do not like. And new leadership in a company may have changed the culture dramatically into a culture that is the right fit for you. Don't count any company out as a possibility in your career future.

TOP TEN REASONS EMPLOYEES GET FIRED

1. Dishonesty, evasion, or lack of integrity on the job.
2. Lying on a résumé.
3. Refusing to follow directions and orders.
4. Talking too much and conducting personal business at work.
5. Inconsistency—unreliable work and behaviors.
6. Inability to get along with other people.
7. Inability to actually do assigned job tasks.
8. Performing tasks slowly, with numerous errors.
9. High absenteeism rate.
10. Drug and/or alcohol abuse.

(Patty Inglish, http://hubpages.com/hub/Fired.)

A FIRING WITH A HAPPY ENDING

A sales planner we'll call Jill, with almost thirty years with a much-admired consumer goods company, recalls the time her company laid her off. She had been a top performer, but a consultant had recommended that everyone in her position be terminated, so she was out. The fact that the termination happened even after all her contributions rocked her temporarily. Jill said, "I went home and had a real pity party. I could not even think that first day." She did all her moaning and self-pitying in private, however. She called a few close friends and reached out to her family for emotional support, but she had the good sense not to talk to any of her colleagues during this process. She allowed herself one very bad day.

The next day, Jill got up and dressed and began her next job: finding a new job, preferably with the same company, which she still loved. She called colleagues in all parts of her company and in different geographic areas. One of the people she called knew of an interview set up for an out-of-state applicant for a job opening. Jill said, "I could do that job and save you the relocation fees." She got the job; in fact, she never missed a paycheck in the transition to the new job in the same company. Jill stresses that no matter how badly you feel you have been treated, you should never say anything but complimentary things about your company. It makes you a more attractive hire. She summarizes several other valuable lessons she learned from this experience:

"I learned that my company does not owe me anything, not even my job. Coming close to losing my job made me value it and the company more. Now, when people are complaining, I tend to think more about the fact that I'd rather have this job, with all the challenges, than not to have it."

"YOU'RE FIRED!"

Of course, few people ever have their employment terminated the way Donald Trump does it in *The Apprentice* TV series. Your exit from a job may be in the company of hundreds, even thousands of others through a downsizing, a merger, a divestiture of a subsidiary, or many other reasons. You may even be given an opportunity to resign, so that the word *terminated* need never be used. Whatever the route to your leaving a company, by following the model we describe next, you can come out of the experience with every dollar, every reference, and every opportunity of value that it is possible to glean from your soon-to-be-former company.

Stage One: The first moments are a B.L.U.R.

The first moments after being let go can be a blur. No matter how prepared you've tried to be for this moment, based on what friends have told you, the actual moment when you are told that you have been terminated can be emotional or at least stressful. So, think B.L.U.R.: it's another handy mnemonic to help you remember how to handle those first moments with grace under pressure.

B = Breathe before you speak. Take oxygen in slowly and deeply. Your brain doesn't function well when you don't breathe, and you may say regrettable things. The shock of this conversation about termination can make you breathe shallowly or even unconsciously hold your breath. Stay calm by purposely breathing as if you were as calm as a sleeping person.

L = Listen before you speak.

U = Understand what is being said to you. Seek this understanding by asking questions. When will the termination be effective? What is the company offering you? You may even ask for some time to digest what has been said to you, but be aware that you may not be given that time. Security issues may require you to leave the building as soon as you are terminated. If an HR representative is involved in the termination, she may have several more terminations to do on the same day and no extra time may be built into the schedule.

R = Repeat to the terminating manager what you think he said to you. Ask for confirmation that you have heard these details correctly.

Stage Two: Bargaining

Realize that you have some leverage, as you have less to lose in some ways than you ever have had in this company. Why would you have leverage? Some companies value their reputation as a great place to work; they don't want you to depart carrying a message of poor treatment—especially if you are going to be active in their industry. Some companies are concerned you might tell competitive secrets or share the dirty laundry of internal politics. Don't ever threaten to do these things, but realize that many companies have selfish reasons for making your exit a win-win.

If your employer makes you an offer that includes severance or other considerations and says you must sign a lengthy, fine-print agreement immediately, with no time to thoroughly read it or evaluate the offer, consider insisting on more time. Not signing the papers at all is also a risk, so decide whether you think the company is going to be ethical in their treatment of you. If you think their offer is probably a fair one, then you might consider signing it without reading every word. At times, the first offer is the best from first-class companies who are trying to make sure people leave with good things to say about their organization. Also, a buyout or severance package may be offered for a limited time or to a limited number of employees. If the offer looks good, you may want to move while the offer is on the table. However, some companies are less trustworthy than others. Are you wary that you will be jeopardizing your retirement benefits or some other valuable asset if you sign without carefully reading the documents? Then you might consider asking for more time, despite the pressure to sign.

As you have little to lose, be bold about asking for some things in a polite and professional way. Often your manager may feel bad or even guilty—deservedly or undeservedly—about letting you go. If he can grant you something you want, he may be inclined to say yes, in an effort to help you make a transition to the next job. What are some of the valuable perks you could acquire in this critical termination conversation?

SEVERANCE. Certainly, severance is at the top of the list of resources you want to walk away with. How much and equal to how long a period differs with each organization. Familiarize yourself with what several other people in your position have received and use that in your negotiations. Knowledge is power. If you ask for a year's severance in a company that has never given more than two weeks' pay, you weaken your position. Be informed for this part of the discussion.

CAREER AND JOB SEARCH COUNSELING AND TRAINING. Many companies offer workshops or even private coaching to help you find the next job. Find out whether your company has retained a consultant to help coach people on their careers; if so, ask for a series of sessions as part of your package. Or find an excellent job search workshop in your area and request that the fee be paid by your company. If you are being terminated by your direct manager, he may not know that HR has a budget for these items, so ask him to check. Conversely, if HR is doing the termination interview, ask HR to request job search support from your manager's budget. One or the other may choose to help you by supplying one or more of the following services:

- Outplacement services
    - Professionally written résumé
    - Seminars and workshops on job searches, interviewing skills, networking, and related subjects
- Career coach

INSURANCE. Ask which of your insurance benefits you can keep for six months. Ask which ones you can continue by paying from your own pocket. In a U.S. company, you will probably be offered the COBRA plan (Consolidated Omnibus Budget Reconciliation Act), but be sure to shop rates. Often you can purchase your own health insurance at a lower rate than you'd pay for the COBRA rates for typically more comprehensive corporate health coverage. This will vary based on your needs and resources and the organization's plan. And don't forget life insurance and disability, if you've had that coverage and those are continuing needs for your family.

COMPANY CAR, LAPTOP, AND OTHER EQUIPMENT. These are some of the costly items the company may provide that you will need to replace immediately so you can conduct your job search. If your company-provided laptop is your only computer, you may find yourself in the position of making a major equipment purchase right now when your cash flow is low. Consider asking that your laptop be made part of your severance package. Negotiate a very good price on the purchase of your company car, if it is not leased. The leasing company may also be open to an offer if you have used the car for over a year.

401(K) PLAN, PENSION MONIES, OR OTHER RETIREMENT-RELATED RESOURCES. You may have paid into some type of retirement account. Depending on whether the company requires vesting, you may be due to receive some of this money, if not all, at this time. Contact your investment advisor or accountant to advise you on the best way to ensure you receive all of the funds due you. If you haven't been keeping your own records of your retirement account activity for the preceding year, obtain copies.

STOCK OPTIONS. Pay close attention to the terms of any stock options you have received. Some expire after termination. Some expire within six months or a year. Exercise your options to earn the most money possible from these certificates. Be sure to ask for an accounting of all options due you and their terms prior to leaving your company.

SEVERANCE AGREEMENT IN WRITING. Don't rely on your memory or the good intentions of your company. Get everything agreed to in writing in the form of a severance agreement.

For each of these perks, try to expand the offer. If the company offers you six weeks of health insurance, try for six months. If your stock options expire in one year, ask for two.

ADDITIONAL PERKS TO NEGOTIATE

Your monthly budget is about to be constrained by reduced income—and the real kicker is, how much more money will you need to spend to find a new job? Can your current company help you out until you find a new job by picking up the tab on some items you may currently take for granted? Consider everything your company gives you that you will now have to provide for yourself. The cost of company-supplied items like a cell phone or Internet service can add up if you suddenly have to pay for them out of your own pocket.

LEAVE A POSITIVE LEGACY FROM YOUR TERMINATION INTERVIEW

We recommend against joking or even bitter farewells like those described in a 2009 AP story:

> *When Jim Neill got laid off, he sent around a farewell email with a subject line designed to get people's attention: "Free food in the employee lounge."*
>
> *Then Neill, who had been with the National Association of Manufacturers for years, left 'em laughing.*
>
> *"These are tough times and with a young family I'm hunting for employment," he wrote, "but you'll be pleased to know I've also begun work on my long-delayed book and instructional DVD . . . 'How to Use Profanity in Every Sentence.'"*
>
> *There's an art to the goodbye emails flooding inboxes as a result of massive layoffs . . . Some are bitter flameouts. Some read like brief memos or mysteries with no explanation of the move; others are like lengthy Oscar speeches thanking coworkers.*

(Kelly Dinardo, "For laid off workers, so hard to e-mail goodbye," Associated Press, March 5, 2009.)

LEAVE A LEGACY

How do you want people to remember you? No matter how angry you are at first or how unfair your termination is, make your departure in such a way that your company and your colleagues will want you back. Close no doors along your career path. Here are some gifts you can give your organization that will make them talk about you—in a good way— long after you have departed:

1. Offer to write a job transition or training memo for the person taking over your responsibilities. You are the most qualified person to train someone else to do your job. What a gift—to your boss, your colleagues whom you supported, and the next person who takes your job! It is not unheard of for the person taking a terminated employee's job to rise in the company and one day be in a position to hire that former employee back, especially if you stay in the industry. Be sure to leave out any critical comments or complaints, as tempting as that might be right now.

2. Particularly if you are part of a larger layoff, offer to serve as a temp or contractor as the company goes through the transitional time after the termination. Remind the person terminating you of your broad knowledge of the company or department, and offer to help in any way if they are shorthanded. This type of contractor arrangement happens all the time with terminated employees. Often, companies lay off key people and then find that they cannot keep up with either the volume or quantity of work with the short staff left. Employees brought

back on a contractor basis sometimes are rehired. Even if the arrangement is temporary, you will have income as you conduct your job search. It is safer to come back through an agency, however, as tax laws are becoming more restrictive about these returns to the workplace. Contact your tax advisor for more information. When you make this offer, the person handling the termination almost always says no; but when the day comes when the department realizes they cannot do everything without hiring some temporary help, you will be the first person they remember because you made this offer.

3. Express your thanks for anything your boss did right. She may not be your favorite person, but she can influence your severance package and perhaps your reference. Mention something specific that you appreciate about her: that you learned so much about the industry from her; that you have become a better communicator because she set high standards in that area; that she was always fair or generous or always supportive of your development.

4. Likewise, say something complimentary about the company. Say that it was a privilege to work for one of the leaders in your industry or for a company that had chosen a niche and excelled in it.

5. You are no longer restricted by the immediate task-focused perspective of your job. If you have ever wanted to make some bold suggestions for change, this is the time. Say what you think should been done next in the position you are leaving, but be sure to say it in a respectful and positive way.

In addition to these strategic moves on how to leave a legacy, Suzanne Lucas, a certified professional in human resources, offers the following ten practical and essential questions you should ask during a termination conversation:

1. *The date your health insurance ends*

2. *Severance amount*

3. *Conditions you have to meet to be eligible for severance (usually there is what is known as a "General Release" you have to sign)*

4. *The date you need to have your paperwork returned to the company*

5. *Any additional obligations on your part—filing expense reports or returning laptops, a BlackBerry, or company documents you may have at home*

6. *Check references: will they simply verify employment or will they give you a positive reference?*

7. *Eligibility for rehire: can you come back?*

8. *If you are eligible to be rehired, what job posting resources are available?*

9. *Can you receive unemployment pay at the same time you are receiving severance?*

10. *Is there any outplacement assistance?*

("The 10 Questions You Must Ask After You're Fired," Suzanne Lucas, *U.S. News & World Report*, July 31, 2008.)

AN OUT-OF-BODY APPROACH TO BEING FIRED

One characteristic of great performers and leaders is the ability to get outside themselves and think beyond their narrow role in the company. They have learned they are not the center of their company's universe. With immense self-discipline, high-performing individuals learn to get out of their own skin and see their performance, role, and results from the corporate viewpoint instead of a more self-centered role. This vantage point allows them to hear feedback or role changes or even terminations with much less emotion. They can think creatively and productively because their thought processes are not constrained by biases and/or clouded by anger or fear.

Joe Ratway of the consulting firm Performance Advantage says that today's focus on one's career and individual success is quite different from the workplace of a few decades ago. Although there are some benefits to focusing on one's career strategy and success, there have been some casualties. An employee can develop tunnel vision about his career and not see or understand changes that are coming for his department or the company. He can become so me-focused that he finds it difficult to accept a good business decision or feedback that may be good for everyone else, including the stockholders. But if an employee can get beyond his own subjective view of his situation, he is immediately empowered. He can respond intelligently, effectively, and professionally. He may come up with an option that saves his job or even improves it.

Developing this high level of objectivity about your company and your role in it is a major career asset. This ability to take a broader view of events, almost like an out-of-body experience, is especially strengthening when you are hearing your boss tell you that your department is being eliminated or outsourced. Different people have different approaches to maintaining this objectivity in stressful situations. Some do relaxation exercises, some meditate, some rely on belief in a higher power, and some mentally role-play that they are a highly confident businessperson they know and simply speak and act as their role model would.

RISKY MOVES TO CONSIDER

In today's tough job market, taking risky moves is not encouraged. A handful of people have tried the following strategies, and a few of them have triumphed. For most people, these moves won't be the recommended strategy for long-term career success. You always run the risk that people in your industry know about your career history, so these steps can possibly make you less attractive as a future hire. Having said that, there's no harm in reading and considering these high-risk strategies:

NEGOTIATE FOR FUTURE VALUE. What do you have to offer your company that they need in the future? Are you the favorite sales rep on a multimillion-dollar deal whose customer adores you—and, more important, trusts you? Offer to work part-time on that deal until it closes, or to work on that deal alone as long as your commission will still be paid. Have you been working on some creative ideas to attract more customers? Offer to finish your report on these profitable ideas—as a consultant. You may even ask to have your time with the company extended while you finish the report. After all, you know the company and the customers better than outside consultants who may come in.

NEGOTIATE FOR A DIFFERENT JOB. Your present position may not be viable for the company, but you may be a great hire for the training or operations department. Ask HR if there is a position elsewhere inside the company.

ASK FOR AN EXTENSION DUE TO EXTRAORDINARY HARDSHIPS. If a U.S. employer understands that having your health benefits terminated will be disastrous for your child with muscular dystrophy or your spouse who has cancer, the company may humanely extend your time with the company until you can find other employment. Each country and each company differ. There is no guarantee, but it may be worth bringing up the specifics of your situation to both HR and your manager, who probably already knows.

Although we do not endorse this strategy, some employees have resorted to threatening to take steps because of wrongdoing on the part of the company. If you feel you are being fired because of some type of discrimination or other bias, you may have a case, but be warned that these battles are long and rarely won by the employee. It is a bargaining point, but not one that proves profitable to the employee in most cases.

A PROFESSIONAL EXIT

You may be asked to complete an exit interview, perhaps on your last day or even by phone. Companies gather data on what elements in their culture can be improved in order to attract and retain the best employees. Although these interviews are touted as completely confidential, you should still be very positive and professional. Throwing your former boss under the bus at a time when you may need his recommendation or help with the transition is just not smart. You can be honest but tactful. Keep your comments objective and not subjective. Don't state opinions or make personal criticisms. Talk about processes, not people.

In summary, it is usually best to leave on a positive note, to position yourself for great recommendations and possible productive networking in the future. The more aggressive tactics are better for short-term success than as a long-term strategy. You will be better served by pouring your energies into making your *next* position a great success than by trying to make your old employer do the right thing.

You may find this termination ultimately leads you to a more rewarding job in an even better company. It happens all the time. Although it is a cliché to say that when one door closes, another door opens, the saying is really true. Throughout a career, setbacks often become catalysts for changing you or changing your circumstances for the better. A termination may be just the push you need to direct you into another industry or a better position that will bring you more satisfaction.

Losing a job that you are comfortable with may feel like a crack in your career, but it may be a way of leading you down a path to a new field for which you have a previously undiscovered gift, a more interesting culture that fits your personality even better, or a difficult but profitable look at some behavior you need to change in order to better engage with colleagues and management. Taking a fresh look at recent events and your last job means being courageous enough to look at what has happened to you and saying, "What is the lesson to be learned from this?"

Ups and downs are inevitable in any career. Responding to the disappointments with poise, grace, and well-thought-out responses can raise your status as a professional in your colleagues' eyes. Show them how it is done by a real professional, and they will remember you the next time a door opens.

7

THE **MOMENT** A **CHALLENGE** TO **YOUR** **ETHICS, LOYALTY,** OR **FUTURE ARISES**

One of the most challenging and defining moments in a career arises when you are asked to do something that is not strictly aligned with company policy—or even with your own code of conduct. Unfortunately, these moments are rarely black and white; rather, they present shades of gray that require you to discern right from wrong. Compounding the problem, the person who asks you to bend the rules is usually either a person you really like or a person who has authority over you—and sometimes both.

Consider the following scenarios. Could what happened to the following employees happen to you?

AN ETHICAL DILEMMA

Bob Yates had successfully served as the sales manager of the western region of a large banking company for just six months. He had established excellent relationships with his employees, customers, and especially his vice president of sales, Don Taylor. Bob had even been able to solve some customer tracking problems and other operations issues that his predecessor had never resolved. All was well until Bob entered his office one day and found a message that he was to see Don at his earliest convenience.

In the meeting, Don asked Bob to do some creative bookkeeping. Don said that he needed $50,000 from Bob's 2008 budget to help finance a mega-event in Las Vegas to entertain customers in 2009. Don knew that Bob had a large budget for training the sales staff. He asked Bob to create fictitious training events and channel the money from those events over to his account to help pay for the customer event. Don explained that this type of switching from one pocket of the organization to the other happens all the time. But he asked that all of this be kept a secret. The sales staff had already been complaining that they were not getting the training they needed. Customers had also made a couple of complaints that the new account managers did not seem to know the products well enough. To officially shift a sum as large as $50,000 from one area of the budget to the next, the budget committee would have to give approval, and Don did not know whether they would understand the value of a mega-event to attract customers.

Don made the point that the mega-event for customers would provide *some* training for the few employees selected to attend. And seeing as features and benefits of the products would be shared at the event, Don felt that it was not much of a stretch to call this a training event and take the money from the training budget.

Don went on to say that no one really tracked training dollars. Because many people went outside the company to all kinds of training-related events, it was hard to monitor how the money was spent, and frankly, company management didn't really care much about training. The training budget had long been considered a resource that the sales division could go to for emergency funds. This was business as usual.

Bob now faced a dilemma. He could not imagine telling his vice president that he could not have the money, which, after all, was in the VP's own organization. Nor did he feel he would be treating the sales professionals he represented fairly if he took the limited training funds earmarked for them and gave them away for more customer promotion. Finally, and most important to Bob, creating fictitious training events as a cover was ethically repugnant to him. Bob felt that whatever he entered into his balance sheet should be true and accurate, and these fabricated events would not be.

A TEST OF LOYALTY

Dee Bolton was being groomed to be the head of the managerial sciences department at a major state university. She had worked many hours both inside and outside the classroom to set herself apart from her peers as the front-runner for the job. She had left a secure teaching position to join this faculty because the dean of the business school had thought he could name a managerial sciences department head the following year. However, budgets would not allow this for another four years. Her relationship with the dean was good, and he clearly valued the work she was doing. But the wait was long, and Dee often wondered whether she was being naive: was the dean really fighting hard enough to get her the position and salary she had expected when she made the switch five years before?

The last two years had been especially difficult. The computer sciences department had suddenly added a managerial sciences requirement. Not enough credentialed instructors could be found on such short notice to cover the additional classes needed. To ensure the quality of the program, Dee was asked to take on the extra classes. She was teaching a double load and doing all the duties of a department head on an instructor's salary. The schedule for the next year had to be made out a year in advance. She had already been told she would be teaching a double load again the following year.

One day, a neighbor gave Dee's name to the dean of a prestigious university who was doing a search for a director of a new program. The program was a perfect fit with Dee's area of study and with the consulting work she had been doing to supplement her current low salary. Dee interviewed and was immediately designated the ideal candidate. As director of the new program, Dee's salary would double. The only catch was that the program was awaiting funding. Although everyone felt that the program would gain approval easily, academic bureaucracy moves slowly. By the time all necessary approvals in the university's system were inked, the new school year would be almost under way. And when it comes to funding, nothing is ever sure. There was an infinitesimal chance that the program and the job could be axed if any last-minute budget cuts took place in the university system. Should Dee risk resigning her current position?

People leave jobs to take new jobs all the time, but Dee's departure would be crippling to the department. Many instructors teach only one or two courses; Dee was teaching four. She knew from experience that finding credentialed instructors for those particular four courses on short notice would be almost impossible. Dee was the de facto leader of this department, and there was no one prepared to take her place. The students would be left in the lurch, and the business school would have a mess on their hands.

So if the funding were approved, Dee would be walking out on her friend the dean and the business school at the last minute. Her resignation would be a shock to everyone, and she knew it would take an emotional toll on her as well, because she loved the students, her teaching, and the program in which she had invested so much of herself.

Dee considered talking to the dean candidly about the other offer, but she felt it might sound like an ultimatum. There was also competition from within her department for the position of department head of managerial sciences. So far, Dee was the front-runner, but would the dean see this consideration of another offer as a breach of loyalty? If the new position were not funded and Dee had to stay, the department head position might go to one of her peers.

IT'S JUST INFORMATION: WHERE'S THE HARM?

Not all theft is of money. It's becoming more common for entry-level employees to be asked to share information with people outside their company. With so much information now available on the Internet, some less experienced employees are tempted to share company information with friends who ask for it. Take the following example:

Mallory worked for a telecommunications company that sent out monthly bills. She had access to the database with names, addresses, and phone numbers of all customers. The company prided itself on protecting this confidential information of their customers. They frequently stated in contractual language that the customer information would never be sold to or shared with anyone outside the company.

Mallory's best friend Terrence from college worked for a stockbroker making cold calls to sell stocks. He asked Mallory to give him a list of names and telephone numbers of residents in their city's wealthiest zip code area. Mallory was sure that no one would find out where the list came from, as she was in and out of that database every day and no record would be created if she copied a few pages. She wanted to help Terrence, who was struggling with his new job because many of the people he was contacting had no money to invest. This seemed like the perfect solution, with no risk to Mallory.

WHAT WERE THEY TO DO?

Early in our careers, we might think people are put into possibly compromising positions because they have done something wrong, but more often it is because they've done something right. This was true in all three examples just described. Bob had been promoted to the sales manager's position and Dee was being considered for department head because they had excelled and achieved. Mallory had been entrusted with confidential information because of her good judgment and technical expertise.

Although it's important to maintain strong professional relationships and a good reputation, professionals must also be looking to the future and their career paths. It is reasonable that even the most dedicated professional would make decisions that are not only good for the organization but also good for him and his family. What does that mean when we're faced with situations like those that Bob, Dee, and Mallory are facing?

People who promote us or have the power to advocate for us often ask for favors or considerations that are questionable. And quite often it is our friends who ask for help that involves bending the rules. Unfortunately, it happens all the time. In Bob's case, however, he is being asked to actually fabricate events, paperwork, and expense accounting—never a good idea, but even less so in our post-Sarbanes-Oxley world. Money is legally shifted all the time from one area of the budget to another without violating any ethical standards. But there appears to be some reason that the vice president can't or won't find a way to do the shifting legitimately. And Terrence's request of his friend Mallory is even more questionable. Let's look at the red flags in all three cases.

RED FLAGS AND CAUTION LIGHTS

There are certain requests that should give you pause to consider a possible ethical conflict:

- You are asked to document or attest to events or numbers that are false or exaggerated.
- You are asked to practice deception that might be embarrassing to you if others in your organization found out. Losing relational capital with your superiors, peers, customers, or those who report to you is as much of a loss as losing actual money.
- You are asked to advocate for something or someone whose value you don't really know. Or you are asked to represent a product, service, or cause that you don't personally know is all it purports to be.
- You are asked to be secretive. Some corporate secrets are legitimate. Is your company launching a new product? You are ethically obliged to keep that secret. But if the secrecy relates to a cover-up or bending the company rules in any way, watch out! Also, if the information will be viewed dimly by another part of the company—such as human resources, regulatory, or safety—take a second look before agreeing to keep secrets.

Bob has all four of these red flags warning him to take a guarded approach to Don's request. Is there a real risk to Bob's career? Perhaps. Could Don be so annoyed at Bob's refusing his support (by not going along with his request) that he does not advocate for Bob's next career move? Yes, but he probably won't, as this would be difficult to explain. Also, Bob is doing a good job, and it is in Don's best interest to surround himself with good people who produce results.

Mallory also should have recognized the red flags, especially the fact that she would face severe consequences if her theft of information were recognized by her employer. In Mallory's case, the theft of information was detected by a fluke. A divorced woman had asked to have her phone service switched to her name, Dale Brooks, from her husband's name, Melvin R. Brooks, III. An entry error was made, and for months afterward her bills came to her in the name of Dale Brooks III. The telephone company was the only service provider who made this mistake. When Dale Brooks started receiving marketing letters from Terrence's investment firm addressed to Dale Brooks III, she knew the source that had sold her information to Terrence's firm. She knew the telephone company had violated its agreement not to share her confidential information. It did not take long to trace the source of the leak. Mallory lost her job and had to enter the job market with nothing to recommend her to a new company but a stony silence when her references were checked.

Dee felt uncomfortable with the secrecy regarding her new job opportunity and subsequent interviews. She knew the difficult circumstances her departure would create for her colleagues and students. As a professional, she felt this was an ethical dilemma.

So if Bob chooses not to agree to Don's request to fabricate training projects in order to fund a customer event, how can he deal with Don effectively? How can he minimize the potential risk and losses? What should he do from the first moment of truth, when Don drops this potentially career damaging bomb in Bob's lap? What could Mallory have done instead that would have saved her job? And how can Dee pursue an intriguing new job opportunity while still remaining committed to her current position?

THE MOMENT THE BOMB IS DROPPED, *DUCK*!

It's a big mistake to feel you must give a clear and complete answer immediately. A hasty response or even a final or definitive response is usually not necessary after such a questionable request. It's easy to get caught up in the moment and start talking, but what you really need is time to reflect. A great mnemonic for handling this awkward moment is D.U.C.K. It reminds you of a possible initial response that will not alienate the person who has made the request. A good first reaction can buy you some time while you figure out a more measured response later. Your goal should be like that of a good doctor: first, do no harm—to the other person's feelings or to your own career.

D = Duck
U = Understand
C = Compliment
K = K.I.S.S.

D = Duck the answer temporarily

Ask for time to figure it out, to study the proposal, to ask more questions. Take all the blame on yourself. Tell the requestor that you are in the middle of a meeting, or that you're so distracted by the meeting you have coming up at 4:00 P.M. that you just need to revisit the request later and get back to him. Buying time allows you to get all the emotion out of your demeanor. It also softens the impact of your answer if it is no. If someone says, "Will you vouch for my project?" and you immediately say no, that is much more damaging to a relationship than if you ask for time and later report, "I have thought about it; I can't do it, and here is why."

U = Understand everything involved

Do this before you give an answer. You may learn things that make this request doable; you may find there is no ethical dilemma at all. You may also find out some information that will make the requestor change her mind about asking you. If you tell the requestor that there is an audit coming up and you are not comfortable doing some task, she may wind up thanking you for the heads-up. Take the time to fully consider and understand every aspect and implication of what's being asked of you. The requestor probably still won't be thrilled that you said no, but you will have treated the request and the requestor with respect.

C = Compliment the requestor

Show consideration for his ego and feelings, which may be bruised if you do not embrace his plans. This is not the time to sound judgmental or morally superior. If appropriate, express something positive like gratitude or admiration that will show that you value the requestor. For example, Bob could have thanked Don for bringing him in on this decision and trusting him. He could assure Don that he understands the confidentiality of the request and will tell no one until they have a better chance to discuss it. Or Bob could have said something like, "Don, you know how much I appreciate your telling me how things are done and how much I have learned from you. I realize that you have been very supportive of me and my career. I just don't want to send any mixed signals at this moment, because I really do think you are the best sales executive I have ever worked with. And I hope you understand that I just need time to take a closer look at this." It is hard to turn down someone who is so supportive and is making a perfectly reasonable request. Don will be less defensive if Bob comes back later and says he just can't go along with the plan to fabricate training receipts.

K = K.I.S.S

This mnemonic-within-a-mnemonic, well established among successful business people, stands for "Keep it simple, stupid." It's a blunt reminder to keep our words to a minimum (even when ambushed). Don't gush or ramble. The less you say in this first moment, the fewer the chances you'll make a mistake. Saying more than you need to can lead to phrases that sound judgmental or critical. Don't give yourself more opportunities to say the wrong things. Trim the number of words you use, and extricate yourself from the situation as quickly as possible. Ideally, you could extricate yourself quickly from the conversation because you really do have a meeting to rush off to and can't say much. If your situation doesn't offer that ideal excuse, you'll need to improvise.

STAGE TWO OF DEALING WITH AN ETHICAL DILEMMA

The D.U.C.K. method will give you an opportunity to ask yourself some good questions, like the following:

- Does an ethical dilemma even exist, or were you worried over something inconsequential?
- What are all of your options?
- Can you ethically agree to part of the request?
- Can you offer a creative alternative to the requestor, perhaps something he has not thought of? Can you help the requestor meet his goals in some other way? Do you have something of value to offer in place of the requested task?
- Will delaying further hurt or help? Sometimes with a delay a problem dissipates. Is that an option?

If you decide that you do have an ethical conflict if you comply with the request, you have some homework to do before having the follow-up conversation with the requestor. First, conduct a cost/benefit analysis on your answer. If you plan to say no, consider all your costs. Could it possibly cost you this job? Your boss's support for the next job? What could the benefits be? Will other people admire your courage? Will the people you manage appreciate your stand? Second, analyze your requestor. If you say no, what reason do you think she will be more receptive to? You may have many reasons for thinking that you should not comply with a request. Most people make the mistake of choosing the reason that is most compelling to them. Instead, offer the reason that is most compelling to the requestor. Will she accept a profit-driven or bottom-line answer better than an answer that expresses concerns over regulatory fears? If Bob tells Don that he can expect productivity to tank if his sales people find out that their meager training budget is being cannibalized, will Don accept this profit-related answer? Would Don be more motivated if Bob told him that an upcoming internal audit is a concern to him? Choose the type of response that will best fit the requestor's priorities.

So how exactly do you say no while preserving a great working relationship with the person whose request you are turning down? You need a beacon of an answer, one that will help you stand up for your principles without casting yourself in a self-righteous light. B.E.A.C.O.N. is the mnenomic for the actual follow-up conversation in which you turn down the requestor's request.

- **B** = Believe in your colleague
- **E** = Express a shared desire
- **A** = Ask, don't tell
- **C** = Collaborate
- **O** = Offer something
- **N** = Never belittle the requestor's values

B = Believe in your colleague

Believe that he has good intentions and that he is asking for the wrong thing for the right motivations. This step is sometimes called "finding the best of the worst." What is *right* about the request? What can you agree with? When you begin your conversation with the person you are refusing, begin with anything in her request that you *can* do. First stress and reinforce all the aspects that the requestor is right about.

E = Express a shared desire
to accomplish the same goals

For example, Bob could tell Don he shares the priority of securing the money to host the mega-event for customers.

Telling Don that he wants to achieve that goal just as much as Don does will alleviate some of Don's anxieties and should lower his stress level a notch. Later, when Bob says he does not think the best course of action is to submit false training receipts, he will not be saying no to helping to find the money. He's clarified that the means and the end are two different issues.

A = Ask, don't tell

Ask the requestor a question or two. Pose these questions in such a way that the requestor may begin to have some doubts that he should even make this unethical request of you. For example, Bob could ask Don whether he knows when the next Sarbanes-Oxley compliance audit is. Bob could also ask whether Don has received the information from the training department that a number of employees have complained that the training budget was cut this year.

As you work together, whenever possible pose your suggestions in the form of questions, not statements. Ask, "Would it work if we did it this way?" Then offer a suggestion. By asking, not telling, you are not trying to push your agenda, and you are treating the requestor with respect.

C = Collaborate

Find ways you can do more together to help the requestor fulfill his needs. Don't try to escape the situation. Simply say you cannot fulfill the need this way; then brainstorm and try to engage the requestor in collaborating with you to see whether there are ways you can help. Don't abandon the requestor right after breaking the bad news to him.

O = Offer the requestor something

Is there something you can sacrifice to help her meet her needs? A sacrificial offer goes a long way toward mending relationships and showing you genuinely want to support a peer or boss to whom you must say no. Bob may not be able to offer training dollars legitimately, but he may have travel money he can offer. What if Bob says to Don, "You know what I could do? I could give you $12,000 out of my travel budget for the travel expenses of employees attending the mega-event. Would that help? Because of the restrictions on training dollars, I will feel more comfortable if you ask the budget committee to approve the move of the actual training dollars over to the marketing and events budget."

N = Never belittle the requestor's values

Never, at any point, question her honesty. Don't compare your beliefs with hers. Be solution oriented and avoid the social and moral commentary. Don't express surprise or disappointment that you were put in this position.

And what could Mallory have said, using the B.E.A.C.O.N. model? The following example is one way she could have handled this situation that would have headed off the damage to her career that she did not see coming:

> "Terrence, I think it's a great creative idea to look at calling areas where money is more available. I see you doing all you can to make this job work, and I want to help you. My contract is very clear that I can't access the database to share confidential information. But what I can do is help you find that information another way. For example, the Patrons of the Visual Arts organization

you belong to may have many of these numbers in your members' phone book. That is just one thing that comes to mind. I have a meeting right now, but would you like to get together Thursday after work to brainstorm some other ideas?"

Is the B.E.A.C.O.N. model a guarantee that no one will be offended when you say no? Absolutely not. Sometimes people's own embarrassment and guilt over making a request that they shouldn't can make them defensive and even hostile. But if you feel you must say no, this is a well thought out and usually successful approach.

SAYING NO IS MORE IMPORTANT THAN EVER

The great issue in management, sales, technology, and every area of business today is trust. Customers, employers, and others are overwhelmed with information and claims of diverse companies and people with statistics and testimonials proving they are the best. Customers make decisions by asking, "Whom do I trust? Everyone's information looks good, but whom do I choose to believe?"

Hiring decisions and technology choices are made in the same way. At some point, there is a leap of faith. Preserving your credibility by making consistently ethical decisions is a must in your career. A history develops around one's reputation, and small decisions accumulate. Learn to say no in a way that is firm but also supportive of the team you work with.

SHOULDN'T WE STATE OUR CONVICTIONS STRAIGHTFORWARDLY?

There are opportunities to state your convictions, and most organizations would be better places if leaders would state theirs more often. The D.U.C.K. and B.E.A.C.O.N. models are not intended to be ways to avoid stating your convictions forever. Rather, they provide an emergency response system you can use to ameliorate an immediate and potentially explosive problem. These models prevent you from saying something that is hurtful to the requestor, your project, and perhaps your career.

Requests to do something unethical are often made under pressure and are often tied to one person's wanting to get specific results on a project that may be in jeopardy. For the success of the department and yourself, you should, if at all possible, take care of making sure the project is a success while maintaining your ethical standards. This is not the time for moral lectures or comparisons of your value system with the requestor's. Take care of business first. The D.U.C.K. and B.E.A.C.O.N. models allow you to continue making progress by working collaboratively with the requestor. The time will come when you can make some constructive observations about ethical choices. While the requestor is under pressure is not that time. You probably would not be very effective, and you might even alienate him and others. Do what you need to do ethically, but leave the moralizing rhetoric for a safer, less combustible time.

MAKING AN ETHICAL STAND

If someone asks you to do something unethical, you will probably want to make your values clear to her at some point. Depending on what feels comfortable to you, you can approach this in many ways. In any case, choose a time when your requestor feels you are supporting her and that things are going well. Casual conversations are best. If comments about your values can be stated in an "Oh, by the way" style, they are more easily accepted than if you preach or moralize. If you find a topic or example in the newspaper and can incorporate it very naturally into the conversation, that works well. The Enron debacle provided endless examples for ethical people to cite in explaining why they make it a practice to never shave the rules in any way.

There are many books about business ethics. If you can find one that is enjoyable to read and reflects your beliefs, keep it on your desk. It will probably draw some comments that could lead to your saying, "This author's beliefs are right in sync with mine. For example, he says . . ." and then share your beliefs. (Do not, however, send this book to the requestor unless he asks for it. That is paramount to an accusation.)

A riskier approach, but one that is important to some people, is to have an offline conversation about the driving force behind your values. If your values are, for example, Judeo-Christian beliefs, then decide whether it is important enough to take the risk of being honest about that influence in your life. You cannot impose your views on subordinates—if you did, it could be grounds for a lawsuit. However, pressure to do something unethical generally comes from those above you in the organization. In a casual conversation with superiors, you may feel you need to say that you pattern your business ethics after the ethics you have been taught in your place of worship. Explain that you'd like to find ways to pursue your passionate commitment to the goals of your organization while not violating your belief system. Again, keep this short and light. Expressions of religious belief are considered off-limits in many workplaces, and you may be running a risk if you bring up your belief system outside of private personal conversations. Still, for some people the risk of constantly being in ethical conflict is so great that they choose to take this risk. And belief systems don't have to be religious; they can be cultural. Again, explaining the source of your ethics and why you are committed to them can be helpful if you feel you have a good relationship with the requestor. If you don't have a supportive relationship with the requestor, these conversations can be much riskier and even detrimental to your career.

BETWIXT AND BETWEEN MOMENTS IN A CAREER CHANGE

There is a difference between being honest and revealing everything you know. You can be honest but still not feel obligated to discuss with your employers opportunities you are pursuing that are not yet solid job offers. Knowing you are waiting for another job offer while others are making plans around you in your current job is no longer considered an ethical lapse. As people change jobs more frequently today, this practice has become increasingly accepted. Another driving factor in relieving you of any guilt over not telling your employer you are job searching or waiting on an imminent offer is that employers broke the employee loyalty contract first through all their downsizings, outsourcing, and offshoring of jobs.

Some employers today think nothing of announcing a merger or departmental consolidation and giving employees two weeks' notice. Employees, in turn, need to live as if this is always a possibility. Employers no longer keep the same employees until retirement as long as they don't screw up. Perfectly proficient employees are terminated every day simply to bolster the company's stock price. All employees should keep an updated résumé handy at all times in case a promising opportunity arises. And just as the CEO is not going to tell an hourly worker that a merger is afoot and his job might be axed, employees are not obligated to tell management all about job offers they've received. Remember Dee Bolton, who interviewed for a new directorship elsewhere while waiting patiently for a promotion from her current position? She had an excellent opportunity to talk to her boss about the possibility she might depart. She chose to tell her boss, for the following reasons:

- She liked her job and felt that knowing another offer was on the table might prompt her boss to advocate for her more strongly.
- This was the perfect opportunity to bring the subject up. Dee was able to tell her boss, "Something unexpected happened the other day, and since the managerial sciences community is a small one I thought I would bring it up to you. I was approached about a job at another university. The job doesn't exist yet—in fact, the program hasn't even been funded—but I wanted to tell you about it. A neighbor of mine from years ago

suggested my name, and the call really came as a surprise." Dee's boss could clearly see that Dee was not out seeking this opportunity and her loyalty was not an issue here. She had taken the opportunity to discuss the possibility so that her boss would not be caught completely off guard later.

Dee was under no obligation to give her organization or the dean a heads-up. But her own value system and sense of loyalty made her feel that being candid was the better course. The obligation to be loyal does not include passing up opportunities to improve one's career and salary. In Dee's case, the dean had breached the loyalty contract first by not delivering on the promised promotion to department head of managerial sciences. Even though the circumstances might have been out of the dean's control, the fact remains that he had induced Dee to come to the school with promises on which he could not deliver.

TAKING CARE OF BUSINESS

Though Dee could not be faulted for taking the opportunity, she could be faulted for her timing. She is obligated to do all she can to leave the department in excellent shape to cover her classes. This called for some succession planning. Dee needed to begin to hire or at least interview part-time instructors who might be brought in on an as-needed basis. She needed to share some of the administrative duties she was handling with some of her peers. If she then had to leave abruptly, people could see that she had made efforts ahead of time to provide resources for the students, the dean, and the

FIVE RULES FOR MAKING AN
UNDERCOVER JOB SWITCH

1. You are not obligated to tell anyone. Based on your values and loyalty, you may choose to tell one or two people. Once one or two people know, it's likely that soon many more people will know.

2. Try to be discreet. Remember that your employer is online trying to hire people just like you and may come across your résumé out there. Services that protect your identity may be preferable.

3. Don't use company time to interview or company computers to apply for jobs or write résumés. Take a half day off or use comp time.

4. Give as much notice as possible to your current employer. However, be aware that some employers will terminate you early if you give them too much notice. For example, if you handle highly sensitive information and give a month's notice, the company may escort you off the premises or give you one week's notice instead. Consider this when resigning.

5. Take care of business before you leave. As soon as you think you may be leaving a position, begin to train others to take over for you. Catch up on filing and leave the work in good shape. Write instructions and even a tutorial for the person who takes your place. You may not believe it now, but many people find later in their careers that the organization they most want to work for is one they left years earlier. It may be ten years later, but if you ever want to return, you want people you left to remember how professional you were. Make your exit every bit as professional as your first weeks on the job.

staff. These steps would go a long way toward protecting her professional reputation.

WHAT TO SAY TO YOUR EMPLOYER

What could Dee have said when her boss was talking about next year's schedule and she knew she might not be there? The following are some suggestions:

1. "I see I am teaching four classes again. I feel we should start to prepare some new part-timers to fill those classes. Since we are in the planning stages, we have time. We need to have some people trained anyway, in case an instructor becomes ill or leaves. By having these instructors pick up at least one of my classes, we will be improving our bench strength."

2. "Do you mind if I ask Jim to help me create the schedule for next year? He is very good at organization, and I think he would enjoy working on it with me."

Might this raise suspicions for the dean? Perhaps. If he confronts her, Dee could say something like "I guess we all get offers from time to time. I don't have a firm offer from anyone, if that is what you mean. I just think it is good to have a team that is not stretched as thin as we are." If the dean presses her, Dee could say, "I do have colleagues who talk to me about openings. So far, it's just talk." And until she has a written offer, it *is* all talk. Still, this type of conversation could bring the appropriate pressure to bear to get Dee named department head. Some of the best promotions are offered when an employee announces that he is leaving to take another job.

Another reason for having this conversation is that if Dee departs abruptly, she could say that she had suggested to her boss that this was a possibility. Her other option is to remain silent and let the students and the dean figure out how to cover next year's classes with very little notice.

CONVERSATIONS WITH YOUR BOSS ABOUT LEAVING

What if your boss hears—or suspects—that you are leaving? A conversation with your boss is in order if you think she may have heard that you are looking for another job. Be sure to communicate face-to-face in as informal a situation as possible. Because you don't want to leave until you've actually secured another job, it is better for you to bring up your employment interests with as little drama as possible. Ideally, you will be talking to your boss about another topic (ideally, a positive one) and the conversation will just casually lead to the job offer you have received. Here are some talking points for this conversation:

1. Be firm that no one has made you an offer yet.
2. Be scrupulous about attendance and not pursuing job-search-related activities on the job.
3. If pressed about whether you are happy with your current job, put your answer in the context of your future. For example, you could say, "I really enjoy the [fill in your favorite] part of my job. Naturally, one day I would like to be a [fill in your goal], but no one is offering that to me. You would not expect me to be in this same role ten years from now. Still, the point at

which I might leave depends on so much. At some point someone may offer me a good opportunity to make a change, but what that opportunity is, I don't know yet. No one can say he will never leave, but I am saying that I won't leave unless it is for a good opportunity."

4. Stress how much you like the company. Mention specific aspects that you value. You may inspire your current employer to make you a better offer. For example, you could say something like this: "I find that the values of this company are similar to mine, and I really like the people. I appreciate the 401(k) plan here with the generous match and stock options. Also, I like our flexible work environment."

5. Be collaborative. Say that you hope you can find a way to be a very long-term employee here if you can find a way to build your salary up or get some exposure in another area of the company or whatever it is you are seeking.

HANDLING DIFFICULT CONVERSATIONS IS A WIN/WIN FOR YOU

Touchy situations related to your leaving a job or being faced with an ethical dilemma are part of being a seasoned professional. The more you face these situations, the more diplomatic you will become and the easier the conversations will be. Whether you feel these conversations turn out positively or not, every difficult conversation you attempt and learn from is building you into the professional you want to be. In that sense, you win whether you get the desired response or not.

8

THE **MOMENT YOU** **RESIGN** FROM A **JOB**

Resigning from a job presents the same opportunities and risks as being fired or laid off from a job. Resigning may offer more opportunities for you than being fired because jobs and networking with the company you are leaving can be even more important to your future. Also, because you are the one leading the change in your relationship when you resign from your former company, you have more responsibility to communicate your departure in a positive and constructive way. There is a protocol to follow, in addition to applying many of the principles from chapter 6. When resigning, because so much is at stake, you have a bevy of reasons to make your exit from a company into one of the most professional acts of your career:

- You may want to return to the company for a different position years from now. The job you have now may not be your dream job, but in five years your current company may have the perfect job for you. Make sure you leave on good terms so that you can return if opportunities improve.

- Your coworkers in your current company may also leave for good opportunities. When their new employers ask them whether they know anyone who would be right for a great position that is open, you want your former colleagues to be able to recommend you enthusiastically. Make sure you leave no negativity in your wake.

- You will always need a good reference from the company you're leaving. Even if you don't list this employer as a reference, companies who thoroughly check your job history may try to contact them. You don't want even a hint of negativity about your work or your final days at the company.

- Your current company may offer you more money or a better position when you resign. It is common for a company to make a much better offer to an employee only when she says she is resigning. Whether it is lethargy or a strategy, many companies don't recognize the consistent high-quality work of good employees. When faced with losing a dependable or gifted employee and when tallying up the cost of hiring and training someone new, many companies will suddenly make a very attractive offer to entice the departing employee to stay.

Grace Freedson of Grace Freedson's Publishing Network tells about her resignation after sixteen years with Barron's Educational Series, a respected but conservative publishing company. Grace had been promoted steadily from a public relations role to senior editor, ultimately becoming acquisitions director. When she realized she had experienced all the growth possible for her there, she left to launch her own firm. Before she left, however, she made sure she tied up all loose ends in a professional way. More than anything, she determined that her attitude during this awkward phase in her relationship with her employer would be positive and upbeat. Grace says, "I was happy there for sixteen years. I grew and developed for a long time before I plateaued as acquisitions director. I determined to focus on the sixteen happy years." First, she gave Barron's a full month's notice so she could help her successor make a smooth transition. Second, she furnished the company with some suggestions for improving her area of the company. She was careful not to be critical but rather to be helpful and extremely positive.

Grace says maintaining this positive style, especially at a tense time such as the exit from a company, was a personal goal. "I think there is too much drama these days: drama over resigning or being fired especially. And people feel they need to vent everything. No, you don't. Did I have any negative experiences in sixteen years? Of course. Everyone does, but you don't need to discuss all the dirty laundry."

SKIP THOSE PARTING SHOTS

In another example, Stephanie (not her real name), a project manager with a mid-size international consulting firm, exceeded every goal set by her company. Clients loved her and consistently asked whether she could be assigned to their companies. The consulting firm often used Stephanie as a bargaining chip when negotiating new contracts. Anyone she had worked for would take on more consulting days and pay for additional consultants if she was assigned to their project. She loved the work and excelled at the job, and the situation was extremely profitable for the consulting firm. Several events transpired, however, that led Stephanie to submit her resignation.

The first such event was the short-sighted decision to offer her a disappointing bonus. It had been the practice of the firm for many years to award semiannual bonuses based on the work that each consultant brought in. Bonuses could be anywhere from a few hundred dollars to as much as $12,000, and this incentive compensated for the long weeks of travel and many late nights that the consulting business requires. In this particular year, however, the company had done poorly financially, due to a sluggish economy. The multimillion-dollar business brought in by Stephanie was among the few bright spots on the balance sheet. When she opened up the envelope and found a check for only $1,000, she was outraged. She was told that she had received the highest bonus given that year, and that most project managers had received no bonus due to the cutbacks. But Stephanie knew the value of the business she had brought in and knew that a bonus check of the usual value would have been a small price for the company to pay to acknowledge her extensive efforts to secure that business.

Second, she became engaged to be married. The dismal bonus had already started her wondering whether life on the road was worth it. She wanted very much to be home more, especially in the following year when she would be married. Stephanie went to her director to ask about a promotion. She asked her director whether, if she were managing and designing the consulting more, perhaps she could travel less. The director, desperately not wanting to lose her great client skills and presence at multiple client locations, said abruptly, "Everyone travels every week. That's the rule."

Stephanie decided that leaving would be the best move for her—personally and professionally. Upon announcing her intention to leave, she did not unleash a parting shot about how she had been mistreated. She simply said, "I am getting married and the travel is not a good fit with my new lifestyle." Instantly, everything changed. One of the partners flew in from New York to the manager's job site in New Orleans. He said the company would be flexible with her about the travel. Stephanie said, "I thought the rule is that 'Everyone travels every week.'" The partner laughed and said, "Don't you think we have the power to amend the rules and redesign a job?"

That was not the only thing that changed overnight. The day after she submitted her resignation, she received an envelope from her director. He said, "We've reconsidered it, and this is your new bonus." It was a check for $12,000. He then said, "We have consultants who have done good work for many years, and we didn't feel we could do more than that now because we can't afford to give it to everyone, but your next bonus will be larger, much larger. In fact, we expect you to set new records for bonuses received." Finally, Stephanie was offered a position several levels above her current job, a sort of mega-promotion. None of these new offerings were considered possible until she resigned her job.

Even though, despite all of this, Stephanie decided to go through with her resignation, she learned a valuable lesson: be courageous when you know your worth. If you offer to resign, be serious about it, because most companies will just take your resignation and show you the door. If your value is great enough, however, you may find yourself receiving a more attractive offer than anyone else in the industry is going to offer you. Your current company may be more aware than anyone of your true value. So for many reasons, you should make an exit that makes your employer and your colleagues hope they have a chance to work with you again one day. It truly is a small world, especially if you decide to work in the same industry throughout your career.

SEVEN STEPS IN A SUCCESSFUL RESIGNATION

Resigning a job requires as much thought as landing a new job. Treat the job and the people you are leaving with respect and take care of your business in an efficient manner. The following are some of the steps to take in a successful resignation:

1. If you are leaving for another position, be absolutely sure you have an employment contract. Don't leave your current position without a solid offer from the new employer.

2. Set the stage. Tie up loose ends, finish projects if possible, solve any outstanding problems in your current position, and discreetly begin to delegate or include colleagues who can step in and handle your job until someone else is hired. If possible, leave on a high note, after a successful conclusion to a project.

3. Tell your boss first. As tempting as it may be, don't tell your best friend at work. If your boss first finds out through the grapevine that you plan to resign, he may take it as an act of disloyalty or may even decide to ask for your resignation. It is extremely rare for secrets of this type to remain secrets, even when your friends have the best intentions. Don't be naive; be discreet.

4. Choose the right time and place to tell your boss. By now, you know whether your boss gets sleepy after lunch or whether Mondays are a particularly stressful day in your department. Find the quietest, most opportune time to talk to your boss. Make an appointment, if possible. Say something like "Do you have some time in the morning to meet with me about some things?" or "Do you have a few minutes to talk after lunch?" You want to make sure you have his undivided attention.

5. Start with something positive about your experience with him and with the department, for example:
   - "You know how much I have learned from you about the brokerage business over the last four years. I think we have done business we can both be proud of and that made the company a lot of money."
   - "The knowledge you have of securities is just one of the reasons I have benefited so much

from working with you. In fact, I have benefited from working with everyone on the team, and I think that is why we have been so successful together."

If you have had your rocky times together, this is not the time to bring it up. The boss may bring it up, but don't take the lead; that would be adding an additional negative to a potentially sensitive situation. If your boss brings up conflict or difficulties, assure him that those are not the reason you are leaving. After all, if a job was highly lucrative, you loved your team, you had a great future where you are, and the schedule was not burdensome, you probably would not be leaving. You can almost always find a way to leave without playing the blame game. In response to your boss's questions about his role in your leaving, it is best to say something that looks forward, not backward:

- "I am leaving because this is an excellent opportunity for me to take on more responsibility."
- "I want to try another industry, to diversify my experience a bit. I may not find another opportunity like this."
- "This new opportunity will help me grow my skills as an analyst [manager, sales professional]."

6. State exactly the position you are leaving to take and the date you are requesting to leave. This will help you keep the conversation objective, concrete, unemotional, and final. You don't want to draw this conversation out. In some cases the conversation will be very brief. In other cases, once your boss accepts the finality of your resig-

nation, he may relax and talk about your time with the company or the recent Yankees hire or the price of oil. You may find it is one of the most enjoyable conversations you have ever had with your boss.

If you have some flexibility about your departure date, you should try to make setting that date a collaborative decision. You could say something like "I would very much like to leave in two weeks so I can take some training I need for my new job. I can transfer all my projects easily in that time. If you don't want me to leave that soon, I could possibly stay another week."

7. Thank your boss for anything he has done for you. This step can take some imagination if you have had a boss who has been sort of a nonstarter for you as a manager or as a role model. Still, you should be able to think of something positive he has done, and your parting remarks should be to thank him. You may not need him as a reference for this job, but your next employer may contact him. Here are some examples of how to thank your boss:

   - "Thank you for teaching me so much about the futures market."
   - "Thank you for all the time you invested in developing me as a manager."
   - "I want you to know that I appreciate all the opportunities (responsibility, encouragement) you have given me here."
   - "I want to acknowledge that if you had not developed my skills, I would not have the opportunity I have now. I just want to thank you for that."

Resigning with no regrets will position you to continue counting on your boss and colleagues as part of your professional network and to solidify your reputation as a credible professional. Review all the considerations regarding benefits and other topics discussed in chapter 6. Resigning the smart way means managing all your resources, including possible vesting in retirement funds or profit sharing.

If you will have a few days (or even months) prior to new benefits taking effect at your new job, find out how much it will cost you to continue your health and other insurance under COBRA or other plans. Usually transient employees can negotiate better prices through temporary insurance plans they negotiate themselves, but always check prices before you opt out of a current program. Existing health conditions like asthma, arthritis, diabetes, or obesity may make it difficult for you to find insurance as an individual. Do your homework before making a decision. Pay as much attention to resigning the smart way as you did to conducting a smart job search. These days, a great deal of money may be at stake.

9

THE **MOMENT CONFLICT ARISES** WITH A **COWORKER** OR OTHER **BUSINESSPERSON**

You may be the most easygoing and considerate colleague in the world, but eventually you will have conflict with someone at work. With any luck, the problem will be short-lived, but if you are working with a chronically difficult person, you may be dealing with conflict for an extended time.

Ev Taylor, vice president of human resources of Regency Healthcare, has been extraordinarily successful in dealing with conflict. He offers this advice for when you are the manager dealing with a situation that may result in conflict, such as a poor performance review or the delivery of bad news. Taylor approaches the employee who may become angry or resentful

AVOIDING CONFLICT

Of course, the best strategy is to avoid conflict in the first place. Here are a few key strategies that can head off conflict altogether:

- Listening attentively and intentionally for both content and underlying feelings and messages
- Pausing to reflect and think about what others are saying
- Doing more than your share of the work
- Following through in order to meet the reasonable expectations of others.

with "intentionality to be respectful." Whether the employee is deserving of being fired or being reprimanded, Taylor's personal goal for himself is to make the experience one in which the employee will realize he was respected throughout the entire process—whatever the outcome. Taylor focuses all his energy and intellect on conveying "genuine positive regard." He says that if he instead relies on intellect and skill, the employee is more likely to become frustrated, scared, or angry. But it is much more difficult for a situation to deteriorate if the employee is being treated with "genuine positive regard."

Taylor also takes responsibility for adapting his behavior based on the response of the employee; in other words, he is flexible rather than rigid. He says, "If conflict arises, the only thing I can change is my own behavior; I know I can't change his. By changing my behavior, I give the employee something different to relate to. It changes the dynamic."

At the executive level, Taylor goes into negotiations or meetings he knows carry the potential for conflict in a calm and assertive way. He goes in with complete confidence that each person in the meeting knows that they are all there to resolve a problem. "I try to go in with my agenda clear, knowing that what we all want is a good decision." This attitude allows Taylor to treat everyone with respect and helps lower tensions and defensiveness around territorial lines.

WHAT TO DO WITH YOUR ANGER

Taylor offers the following advice when you are in the position of the subordinate being given upsetting feedback by your boss:

> *"I try to keep my agenda clear. As I listen to the feedback that may seem unfair or unfounded, I remind myself of what the real agenda is. The real agenda is not my selfish one to defend myself or show I am right. The real agenda of the person giving me the unpleasant feedback and my agenda are to come up with a successful solution. I listen to the information and try to see how it can be a contribution to the success of my company or to resolve a problem in a collaborative way. If I can discipline myself to set aside my agenda and hear the suggestions and feedback as steps in a possible solution, I can deal with the information much more effectively."*

Finally, Taylor reminds us all that the only behavior one can change in a conflict is one's own. By changing your behavior (as we'll discuss shortly), you change the whole dynamic of the negative communication. No amount of reasoning or information is likely to cause an antagonist to back down in the midst of conflict. An about-face on your part, however, may change the entire tenor and tone of a difficult verbal exchange.

PERSONALITY TYPES: A KEY TO UNDERSTANDING OTHERS

It's also helpful to realize there are personality types that are radically different from yours. These differences may seem strange and their manifestations even rude to you, but they are actually just style differences. There is no one right business communication style. A diversity of personality styles, like every other type of diversity, can actually improve your department's performance results. Still, coexisting with another employee whose style makes you uncomfortable can be wearing. It helps to gain some understanding of personality styles.

Most studies of personal style differences are based on the work of the influential Swiss psychiatrist Carl Jung. Although this is something of an oversimplification, there are four primary communication styles. The Personality Style Table (see pages 170–171) presents my own contemporary names for the four styles and an overview of each.

As you can see from the table above, each style has value but also has a trait or two that could drive teammates crazy. A great strategy for avoiding conflict is to see these annoying or nonproductive habits as differences in style rather than as failings or unwise choices. For example, an analytical person may have spent months studying a new plan for delivering materials to construction sites. He has worked out all the details and corrected flaws to help solve a current problem of the sites going without materials for days at a time and thus hindering productivity. Three days before the new plan is to go into place, a staff meeting is held. The analytical type does a presentation of the final details of the plan, which the whole team has been aware of for months. At the end of the presentation, the creative idea person says, "Or, we could do it this way . . ." He begins to detail an impractical, unproven, unresearched idea that has just occurred to him.

The analytical person is furious. He feels that the creative idea person has just sabotaged his plan and his presentation. He sees the new idea as an impediment to implementing the plan he has worked so hard on. The attack feels personal; the analytical employee feels the idea person has intentionally shown disregard for the excellent plan put forward and for the analytical person's hard work. The analytical type feels the spontaneous outburst was irresponsible and the idea is stupid.

If the analytical employee understood the style of the idea person as described in the Personality Style Table, he could see that the attack is not on him personally or on his idea. It is the innate nature of the creative idea person to constantly brainstorm and share top-of-mind ideas without really thinking them through. And he should not be stopped. It is through this spontaneity that new and innovative ideas come forward, so idea people must be allowed to think out loud this way. That does not mean that all their ideas must be accepted. In this case, the need for safe, reliable material delivery would probably mean that the analytical person's idea would be implemented, but the analytical employee and rest of the team should listen to the idea person's thoughts.

Learning to watch the other personality styles act out their differences and accept them as different, not wrong, is key to

PERSONALITY STYLE TABLE

POSITIVE FEATURES	POTENTIAL PROBLEMS
THE STRAIGHT ARROW	
Honest Clear about opinions Efficient Takes initiative Leadership Good time manager Productive	Blunt May unintentionally hurt others' feelings Insensitive Not always the best team player Has tunnel vision about how to do things May not trust those who aren't straightforward
THE EMOTIONALLY OPEN	
Good listener Builds intrateam relationships Supportive Notices people's needs that may be overlooked Can bring fun and social element to team Helps others through stressful times	May be too sensitive Can cloud judgment with emotion May emphasize problems that could just blow over May demand time-consuming attention to people issues

maintaining harmonious relationships in the workplace. It is easy for the analytical type to think the creative idea person is wrong for interrupting with a sketchy idea that is impractical to implement. It is easy for the creative idea person to see the analytical person as boring, old-fashioned, and closed-

POSITIVE FEATURES	POTENTIAL PROBLEMS
THE ANALYTICAL	
Detailed planner Identifies problems Cautious Prevents mistakes Prepared Provides documentation Credible Trustworthy	May have analysis-paralysis Avoids risk Uncomfortable with change May slow progress and initiative Caught up in details instead of main points May seem negative
THE CREATIVE IDEA PERSON	

Good time manager
Innovative
Creative and artistic
May see future trends and
   opportunities
Source of new products, features,
   and services
Unique
Can aid in branding and
   differentiating
Make great change agents
Encourages risk
Embraces technology and new
   methods
	May be too far out
	Has difficulty finishing projects
	Changes mind too often
	Seems inconsistent or flighty
	   to some
	May contradict self and forget
	   previous ideas
	Is easily bored
	Less interested in the ideas of
	   others than in own ideas
	Likes change for change's sake
	May be impractical

minded. Both need to realize that the other is not wrong, just different—stylistically different.

Each of us operates in all four styles every day, but we tend to operate in one style more than the others. Think about the members of your team. Can you identify which style each one tends to operate from most of the time? Is one person clearly the straight arrow or the emotionally open type?

Try to be more attuned to the nuances of the personality in front of you and less judgmental. Instead of saying the person is wrong, uses poor judgment, or is annoying, try to figure out what he is doing based on his personality style. Then try to appeal to that style by adapting your own. With the emotionally open person, be friendlier and ask more personal questions. Get to the point and be direct with the straight arrow colleague. Ask the creative person to brainstorm with you and ask what her ideas are as you share your own. Finally, bring lots of documentation and an agenda when you communicate with the more analytical people you encounter.

Switching to better communication

Joe Ratway, owner of the performance consulting firm Performance Advantage, says that stopping to make yourself look at a situation differently is part of professional maturity. He says employees need to learn to "toggle a switch" internally that will help them change from seeing the current situation only from their viewpoint and to see it from the other person's view.

According to Joe, when your boss or someone in another department is not giving you what you need, it's helpful to step back and ask yourself, "I wonder how hard his job is?" As you begin to think about all the pressures, goals, and problems that are constraints for the other person, you can begin to work with that person more effectively. That doesn't mean you always back off and accept less than great support, but you can begin to collaborate with more empathy.

Based on working in many organizations, Joe says that those who shine have the ability to separate their personal, subjective feelings from the organization's or department's needs. These exemplary performers can gain clarity very quickly and see what the good business decision would be in a situation, even when it means personal disappointment to them. It takes courage to make yourself vulnerable enough to drop your self-oriented side of an issue and be open to seeing the broader picture, knowing you may lose some short-term battles. But there can be huge long-term rewards for being able to be this objective. You will make better decisions, and you will be perceived as a person worth investing in because you take feedback and organizational changes and grow both personally and with the company. Demonstrating that you can adapt to change and grow into positions of greater responsibility is crucial to your advancement. Even if you don't agree with all business decisions, you can prove that you can thrive and be successful even under difficult circumstances.

Unfortunately, some employees persist in personalizing business decisions that are not aimed at them. Younger employees, especially, can become so centered on their own careers that they can't see the larger, overall company view of what needs to be done. Such employees do not display professional maturity—and they pay the price. Most colleagues and managers are repulsed by employees who are flagrantly me-centric.

PACE YOURSELF

Grace Freedson of Grace Freedson's Publishing Network has a unique take on the reasons for conflict. She theorizes that technology is to blame for how people increasingly "fly off the handle, causing conflict in the workplace." Grace says that with the rapid rate at which information comes at employees now—it's become the norm to respond immediately by email or text or even Twitter—mistakes are inevitable. People read things incorrectly, phrase things carelessly, react rashly, and just generally move too thoughtlessly in their haste. Clashes and conflict are an inevitable result of our frenetic pace. We are hurtling headlong, trying to return every email and text by day's end, and the needed quality and thoughtfulness of the response may suffer.

You cannot slow the pace around you, but you can control your response to the events—if you pause, take a breath, and think through the best way to communicate through the issues. Taking a moment to decide whether you will handle the conflict on the spot with diplomacy or escalate the issue can make all the difference in how successful you will be this week—and maybe for a long time to come.

WHEN YOU CAN'T AVOID CONFLICT

The following strategies are some of the ways you can deal with conflict once it breaks out.

Going to the top?
Should you go to your boss to help you with a conflict or problem? This is like asking what the price of a three-bedroom

house is without knowing whether it is an upscale, luxury home in Marin County or a fixer-upper in a rural county in South Dakota. It just depends.

If possible, solve problems at your own level. That is why your boss hired you. If he has to make the hard decisions, then he is doing the heavy lifting. Still, there are times that your manager's experience or power can resolve a problem faster and more easily than you can. One sales manager I interviewed said she involves her manager more quickly than she once did. "I communicate my issues, but I have a rule. I never go to my boss with a problem without also articulating to him what I think the solution should be. I will tell him all possible solutions, but let him know the one I am leaning toward." This is good advice. Lending clarity to the problem and suggesting options for solving it makes your manager's role much easier, and he will be much more eager to help you.

Focus on process, not people

Dr. Robert Warner of Atlanta is a cardiologist and member of the Wellstar board of trustees. He has served in many positions of responsibility in top hospitals as well as having run his own professional corporation. Dr. Warner's advice when facing a workplace problem is to focus on process rather than people. He offers the example of a mistake that he recently caught—a mistake that could have harmed one of his patients. It involved a new, state-of-the-art piece of equipment purchased by the hospital. A nurse apparently made a mistake in using the new equipment. Although in that moment some doctors would have focused on the nurse and played the blame game, Dr. Warner had a greater focus: to fix the problem. He went to the chief of staff immediately to halt the use of the equipment until the problem could be resolved, thus avoiding similar risks with other patients. He also went to the head of nursing and discussed the problem with her. He was not at all accusing of the nurse; instead, he explained that he felt that the nurses had not been given the training they needed to adapt to the new equipment. The head of nursing agreed. She said, "I tried to tell my management that our nurses needed more training, but I did not have the power to make it happen. Since you are on the board, maybe they will

EIGHT WAYS TO AVOID CONFLICT

The following are some tried-and-true guidelines for heading off or resolving conflict:

1. Most people respond best to concrete, vivid language. If you are vague, misunderstandings can occur.
2. Be very clear as you express your desire to understand and to resolve the issue.
3. Maintain comfortable eye contact and try to have a pleasant facial expression.
4. Concede the small things. Focus on the important issues and don't get bogged down in minor errors of thinking or detail.
5. Give lots of examples, especially from your life. Don't use examples from the other person's life or you may seem critical.
6. The word "you" is almost everyone's favorite word when you are complimenting and enjoying camaraderie. Drop this word like a hot potato when you are discussing controversial topics that could

listen to you." She was right. Within a week, the vendor had training sessions set up at the hospital to remedy the problem.

A potentially life-threatening problem was solved because Warner did not focus on the person who made the mistake but instead took a thoughtful look at the process. He then reached out to the parties involved to get everyone collaborating in the solution. Warner says, "I have headed up many teams and served in executive roles in my practice and also in the larger Wellstar organization. The way I get things done is

lead to conflict. If you use "you" in a conflict-laden conversation, the tone can sound accusatory. And definitely don't use the royal "we," as in "We don't do things like that around here." A similar condescending pronoun is "one," as in "One should not accept such policies."

7. Engage fully with people if they are trying to work out a conflict with you. Answer questions simply and clearly; don't be evasive. Don't say, "That's all right" or "If you say so" or other phrases that are cop-outs for engaging.

8. Don't remotely question another person's values or reasoning or you may sound challenging. Speak in terms of what is and not what might be or what you guess. Avoid making people defensive by asking questions that require they explain themselves. Asking someone why he thinks as he does seems to question his judgment or his right to think differently.

through consensus and collaboration. I can come up with better solutions that way and people enjoy going to work in organizations run this way. Most decisions are not black and white; more viewpoints can give me the shades of gray to make a good decision." The following is another type of measured approach to resolving conflict.

SOLVE IT QUICKLY

Finally, when it comes to conflict resolution, sooner is better than later if at all possible. Addressing conflict while the problems are minor may aid in preventing a spark of conflict from erupting into a roaring blaze. Although avoiding conflict remains the best strategy, staying objective and thoughtfully phrasing your responses will go a long way toward resolving the problems with colleagues, customers, and other business associates.

10

THE **MOMENT** **YOU** ARE **RECOGNIZED** FOR **EXCELLENCE**

$\mathbf{S}$ pecial moments will come along in your career, and you should enjoy them. Savoring success is important after you have worked hard to receive a compliment, a pat on the back, recognition, or a reward. Don't forget, however, that these moments are some of the most important ones to leverage and to use to build your career and your reputation. You will want to offer appropriate responses and communicate effectively in such moments. Consider the following scenarios that could very possibly be in your future:

- **Honors and performance awards.** Today is the staff meeting when your boss will announce who receives the Golden Laurel Award, given each year to the employee who has outperformed peers and made extraordinary contributions to the department and the company. Much to your surprise, your name is called out. What do you do next?

- **Promotion.** You have just emerged from your manager's office, where she has told you that she has been promoted and that she has chosen you to take her place. It is a huge promotion for you. To complicate things, two of your peers have more seniority with the company and are probably expecting to be named the successor. What is your next step as you pass by the cubicles of your more senior colleagues?

- **Acknowledgment or award for innovative or exceptional contribution.** You have submitted an idea to your company's Innovation and Corporate Entrepreneurship program. You receive an email telling you that your idea, which will save the company $3,000 yearly in data storage, has won a prize of $500 and acknowledgment from the CEO. You are the only one in the department who receives the email. How do you communicate your good news?

- **Media attention and industry exposure.** A regional business magazine does an annual edition on "Ten Outstanding Young Professionals to Watch." Everyone in your business community reads this edition of the magazine each year. You have just received a phone call that you will be one of the ten professionals featured in the magazine this year. How do you prepare yourself and others for this event?

- **Pay raise.** You are one of seven senior aerospace consulting engineers. Your work for Delta Airlines has won you many accolades from that complex client. Your boss calls you in and tells you that he is giving you a pay raise that will make you the highest-paid individual contributor in the company, because of the valuable work you have done and your willingness to go beyond expectations to solve problems. "This is so cool," you think. With whom can you share the news?

Variations on these scenarios could happen to you during your career. Your first inclination may be to do what you would have done in high school—run out and breathlessly tell all your best buds! As much as we believe in celebrating these moments, if your best buds are your coworkers, slow down and take a breath before you say anything. Even though your coworkers may be happy for you, some may not be able to help stop themselves from comparing how you have been acknowledged to how they have *not* been acknowledged. Each of us has our own slant on how valuable our contributions have been. Diverse contributions are not rewarded exactly equally in any company and any department. Also, the company may place a much higher value on a particular strength—say, interpersonal skills, whereas one of your unacknowledged colleagues may have invested all his time and energy in technical skills. The employee who is more technically proficient may judge you only by your ability to perform technical tasks and thus may not see what the company values in your contribution.

Also, some professionals do a better job of marketing their contributions inside the organization and thus may be better rewarded than those who pay no attention to managing this aspect of their career. From this pool of people who do not skillfully communicate their value to the company to higher-ups, you may encounter some surprising responses to your good news. For each of the scenarios just described, you can take strategic steps that allow you to share your successes appropriately and professionally with colleagues and the people who can help you get that next award or promotion.

HONORS AND PERFORMANCE AWARDS. When you are given an award in a meeting, you must strike that balance between being joyous and appreciative and being smug and arrogant. And you must be intentional about not appearing smug and arrogant, as employees with low self-esteem may want to believe the worst. Here are the steps to take when the award is announced:

- Smile and thank the person most responsible for the award and also the person presenting the award. Be sure to establish eye contact as you do this. If appropriate, shake hands. When a manager has looked forward to awarding an honor on an employee for outstanding performance, it's a letdown to see a negative response when the big moment comes. When employees, often in a display of false modesty, shrink back and make faces and roll their eyes, as if to say, "You mean I have to embarrass myself by walking to the front of the room?" this is not a gratifying response to the manager bestowing the award. Also unattractive is a sarcastic or wiseacre remark about the award or the wisdom of choosing the employee. This is not modesty; this is rudeness.

- If you are asked to say a word or two, keep it short. Talking too much will reinforce the idea that you are full of yourself. In your remarks, acknowledge three groups of people: all the worthy candidates, the team and allies that earned the award for you and with you in a team effort, and your boss and other management who supported you. Say that you are touched, surprised, and honored. Then say a simple thank-you and sit down!

- When you return to the office, if colleagues who were passed over talk to you, never say you were undeserving or that you think they were more deserving. You can say, "I just wonder what the criteria were, because I know your work on the MaxxPass project was also highly valued." If you compliment a colleague, be sure the compliment is very specific about a project or task they did well. Otherwise, you could sound patronizing.
- Send personal thank-you notes to anyone who contributed to your success: your boss, your support people, and key teammates. Send these within a day or two of receiving your reward. It is hard to be resentful of a winner who humbly thanks you.

PROMOTIONS. When you are promoted, you should never be the first to communicate the news to colleagues. Your boss should. If she doesn't, draft an email for her and ask her to share the news with others so that you do not have to be the one to tell your colleagues. Or ask her when she will be announcing it in a staff meeting. Promotions can be tricky, as you may now be in a role that changes your dynamic with your colleagues. They may have a direct or dotted-line reporting relationship with you now. You need to have an intentional, but friendly, conversation with these people as soon as possible. If you are friends, invite them to lunch, coffee, or a baseball game. Early in the outing with them, say, "I hope our new reporting relationship isn't going to be awkward for you. You know I respect your work." Bring it out in the open; allow them to talk about it; open the door to talking about it in the future.

Early in my career I made the mistake of not doing this. In the management consulting firm I was working for, I was promoted into a management position above my colleagues. They were especially resentful as I was the only one without an MBA. What I did have was the ability to communicate and negotiate very effectively and positively with top executives, a skill required in the manager's job I was promoted to. My first six weeks on the job were rocky. Malicious compliance and lack of respect were rampant. These formerly friendly colleagues really wanted to see me fail, to prove their theory that I was not the right person for the job.

Finally, I decided to take the steps I should have taken on day one of my promotion. I discreetly arranged to have time alone with each colleague. I told each one that I understood that with their qualifications and experience they thought they should have been chosen instead of me, but my promotion was the choice of management and the hand we both had to play out. I told them I understood their disappointment over this position, but there were many promotions and opportunities in their futures. I promised that if they would work with me and be successful in their current role, I would actively search for opportunities for them, not just in our department but across the company.

I then thoroughly interviewed them about their career aspirations and their interests. We were working at that time in the areas of performance development, training, and corporate culture. It turns out that many of them were not really interested in this area of the company. They were much more interested in working in accounting or operations. I promised to begin cultivating contacts in those areas so I could find out about new opportunities for them in the fields they truly enjoyed.

The turnaround after these conversations was remarkable. The employees made our department extraordinarily successful. And as I began to find great professional opportunities for them, one by one, in other departments, their loyalty to me and to the company increased exponentially. The key was to communicate openly and to demonstrate sincere interest in them and their professional growth and aspirations. Those conversations also took the focus away from me and onto their personal success and performance.

Randy Lyle, former president of Georgia-Pacific Shortline Railroad, tells of becoming a branch manager when many of his friends were not being similarly promoted. He continued to stay in touch, just as he always had. When friends made remarks like, "So now you are a big shot," Randy would just laugh, as if the term *big shot* was an unlikely description of him. He maintained his friendships by not taking himself or his new position so seriously, as well as not taking his old friends for granted. Randy took it upon himself to reach out, stay in touch, and maintain his friendships.

ACKNOWLEDGMENT OR AWARD FOR INNOVATIVE OR EXCEPTIONAL CONTRIBUTION. Occasionally in a career, a person performs a feat or comes up with an idea that is so exceptional, he creates a lot of buzz and draws attention to himself. The person who is acknowledged may not be the hardest worker or the most senior employee, yet he has serendipitously come up with something that the company values, acknowledges, and perhaps rewards. As companies become more aware of the revenue value of entrepreneurship, we will probably see more awards or bonuses given for efforts like this.

Even the smallest companies recognize initiative in direct or indirect ways. A small local lumber company was owned by a man who realized that one of his employees had some great ideas for attracting and keeping new customers. To encourage this employee and others, the owner would annually give plaques and awards for sales, new ideas, and professionalism. When the owner retired, instead of selling the business, he made the young employee his partner. The young employee built the business from small to mid-size, and in the process he made himself and the former owner very wealthy men.

If you are the recipient of such an award, the announcement, of course, should come from the company or from your boss. If you have submitted an idea to a company contest or program that awards innovation, you should have already told your boss what you have done. Your winning the award should not come as a total surprise to your boss. Even worse, your boss should not have to find out from another manager after you have already been notified. You should share the information with your boss immediately.

In conversations with your colleagues, focus on the problem that was solved rather than on the award. Say, "I just knew that we were all very frustrated with the inability to print color copies from our local office and that waiting for color copies from corporate was costing us marketing opportunities. These low-cost desktop units looked like the ideal solution, so I just submitted it." Again, the emphasis is on the workplace problem solved and not the glory of your recognition, what was said to you by the CEO, the prize money, or whatever. Focusing on problem-solving reinforces your image as a team player and not a glory-hog.

MEDIA ATTENTION AND INDUSTRY EXPOSURE. Some up-and-coming professionals just attract more positive media attention and industry interest than others. Your company may view you as the type of professional who projects a positive image for the company and may send more opportunities your way. You may even be actively seeking positive media attention as a career strategy, and that is a smart idea. For whatever reasons, you find yourself receiving more media attention than your colleagues. You can probably count on at least one of these colleagues thinking you are a showboat, a big-hat-no-cattle worker, or a dangerously ambitious person who could be a threat to their personal ambitions. With these folks, you will need to work hard at building trust and credibility as a team player and an ardent supporter of their efforts.

More relevant to your career is the opinion of your boss. In his case, you will have to show that the work and the achievement of departmental goals are more important to you than the hype about your work. You will need to demonstrate by your actions and professionalism that you are fully engaged in your current role and not distracted by looking for future career opportunities. You still need the boss you have now to endorse you, recommend you, and help compensate you. Take care of that relationship before you take care of outside media opportunities or networking meet-and-greets. The following tips on the next page will help you gain the most from your season as a media darling without damaging the vital work relationships you need to be successful in your current job.

- As in the scenarios described earlier, be sure you give credit to your colleagues and boss when you are interviewed. Robert Woodruff, who built the Coca-Cola Company into the mega-giant it is today, said, "You can accomplish anything you want as long as you don't care who gets the credit." That is bankable career advice. Phrase the credit you give others in quotable sound bites, like, "I could not have reached this goal without a supportive and savvy manager who guided me," or "Getting the right people on the team was what made the difference and Gail Brown, our director of recruitment, hired just the right people."

- When asking for time off, never be assumptive or pushy. Ask politely and acknowledge the investment your boss will be making in you.

- Give others some of your opportunities. Suggest that the interviewer get a quote from your boss or a colleague.

- Be relentlessly positive. Dealing with the media is no time for thinking through problems out loud or being candid about your company's flaws or your own. Taken out of context, these quotes can be damaging. You may think you are being candid with a reporter with whom you have developed rapport, but remember they are professionals at making people feel comfortable enough to dish the dirt.

- When complimented, say a sincere thank-you, then shift the focus from you personally to a company goal, project, or another employee. Thank the person or say, "Oh, did you see that?" and then mention another article that has come out about your company. Make it clear that it is not about you. Shift the conversation to the project or department highlighted in the article. Say something like, "I hope it gets us support for the expansion we need to fund"; then start talking about the expansion.

- Be careful about sharing specific information with the media. Also, be prepared for loaded questions that might trip you up and lead you to say something that sounds negative. You might want to meet with your boss prior to any interviews to discuss some positive messages you should try to plant, some topics to avoid, and some ideas for sidestepping touchy issues. If your company is sometimes criticized in the press for something, develop with your boss some neutralizing responses to use when you are hit with these unpopular topics. For example, has your company been criticized for building a fabulously expensive new facility and then raising rates? Is there any litigation against your company that the public knows about? Any safety issues? Has the company been criticized by the labor unions for low wages and then posted huge profits? For issues like these, prepare some positive messages ahead of time.

One way in which rising professionals gain industry and media exposure is through professional organizations. Many employees have found excellent training in industry knowledge through these organizations. Some companies even encourage employees to participate and become officers in order to increase the company's visibility in the industry and to bring back ideas about industry trends. But sometimes managers begin to regret ever approving a day for an employee to attend a meeting, because it turns out to be the start of a spiral of more and more meetings and distractions. An employee may begin to do more work for the organization, often on company time. If a professional becomes an officer of the organization, he will usually need more days off to attend planning meetings and regional and national conferences. The employee may even expect the company to pick up the tab. Imagine the manager who at first thought he was approving a one-day conference at a nearby hotel now being asked to pay travel expenses to an out-of-state national conference and a regional conference two hundred miles away, not to mention the extra six days of work missed by the employee who is now the secretary of the organization! Once burned like this, some managers institute a policy that employees pay their own dues and use their own vacation days for such meetings.

What are some rules you should follow to make your participation in professional organization work for you and your boss?

- Discuss with your boss your decision to join a new professional organization. Ask for her advice about the organization that would make you more valuable to the team. If she is involved in the decision, she will be more supportive.

- It is even more important to ask your boss to advise you before you run for office. Ask about the pros and cons vis-à-vis your job. Mention that you are considering running as a developmental move to improve your presentation skills or your organizational skills or your industry knowledge. Some managers are always looking for steps to write into employee development plans, and your experience as an officer may offer a tangible developmental step that could be included.

- Plan and complete all assignments ahead of schedule if you are going to be out for a meeting. Be more than caught up; be proactive. Make sure that your absence does not hinder the productivity of the department.

- If you sense your boss does not want to offer you time off for meetings, offer to take some personal time along with the time off you are requesting. In other words, if your organization wants you to attend a two-day conference, offer to take one day of vacation time and one day that is given by your company. Your willingness to invest will be persuasive.

- After every meeting or conference, write up a report or email bullet list of what you learned that is of value to you as an employee and/or to your organization. Knowledge transfer has value, and your boss needs to be updated as well.

- Be sure to say thank-you and to mention what developmental changes you are experiencing through your participation.

PAY RAISE. This one is easy. It is no one's business how much money you make. Of course, you should not say so this bluntly, but that is the bottom line. Naturally, others may find out how much you make in all kinds of ways, but you should make it a practice not to discuss bonuses, salaries, or other compensation with other employees. This is to help you and to make your boss's life easier if he decides to reward you and not someone else. If another employee tries to draw you into a conversation about this, laugh it off and disengage quickly. If the person persists, just say, "I made it a policy a long time ago not to discuss finances and pay with business associates. I hope you understand, it's nothing personal."

POST-SUCCESS STRATEGIES

An executive of a top international investment firm recently told me that the greatest surprise he received when he became a leader in his industry was how many people there were who were as bright and innovative as he is. He had been a genuine wunderkind, always at the top of his class or department, up until he reached the executive level. He found it humbling to know many people were just as brilliant as he is.

He also said he came to realize that after you come up with a great idea, you can't simply coast on it for very long. Among successful executives, launching the latest great idea means the start of looking for the next great idea. Sam Fitts, the former number-one sales professional with Federated Department Stores, says that the time to make a sale is on the heels of a sale. Many outside sales professionals often want to take a break as a reward after making a sale; this is wasting the momentum, according to Fitts. Something about the success of the previous sale will communicate to customers and increase your confidence and magnetism for making the next sale and the next. Whether you are dealing with technology, merchandise, or internal operations, ideas will be copied and proliferated. Fresh new ideas become so yesterday in a short amount of time. Executives must be visionaries and continue to look for innovation and creative approaches.

ENJOY YOUR SUCCESS

If you are reading this chapter, you are already successful or are preparing yourself to be successful. Don't forget to celebrate with your family, neighbors, and friends. Savor the moment and acknowledge every milestone with a dinner with a supportive friend, a small splurge for yourself, or a toast. The strategies in this chapter will help you fully enjoy that success and minimize any issues that sometimes come along with being acknowledged and rewarded. What a good problem to have!

CONCLUSION
GAME PLAN FOR REAL LIFE COMMUNICATION: SIX MODELS FOR YOUR FUTURE SUCCESS

You are now armed with the information and strategies for saying just the right thing to anyone at a make-or-break moment (and any other time). Executives at any level will not intimidate you, because you know the topics and approaches to use with them. Bring it on!

Still, you may be asking yourself, "I know all about what to do—now what do I do to bring about those make-or-break moments? How do I get started right away to make my future more successful? I don't want to wait until opportunities happen to me; I want to make them happen!"

And that is exactly what you should do.

One way to learn to be successful is to look at what the most successful people have done and pick out a few things you want to emulate. This chapter shares insights into some of the most exciting stars of our time in business, technology, politics, and the arts. You won't necessarily want to be *exactly* like the heroes described in this chapter, because their style may not be your style, but they definitely did some things right, and those are the things you should consider worthy of emulation.

The following people are either geniuses, brilliant risk takers, or the luckiest people on earth. Whichever conclusion you draw, be intentional about studying what they did that will work for you. Take notes. Ask yourself how the things they did to catapult themselves to success can work for you in your job or your industry.

JACK DORSEY, COFOUNDER AND CREATOR OF TWITTER

Jack Dorsey has already employed many of the strategies this book advocates. He was relational, as described in chapter 5, which details how to become accepted and valued by your team wherever you work. Because he was relational, Dorsey wanted to stay in touch with all his friends from various parts of his life and from previous workplaces. At the time, Dorsey was assigned to work on software to help taxis and buses stay in communication with the dispatcher with real-time information. Not only were these communities of taxis or buses communicating with a single source—the dispatcher—but they also were letting other taxis and buses know what they were doing and alerting them to issues that were coming up, moment by moment. An idea began to take shape in Dorsey's mind. How could he create a similar software to stay in communication with his friends?

Dorsey's desire to share the current information in his life with his friends led to his invention of Twitter, the latest greatest communication phenom that cuts across email, text messaging, and blogging, to name a few. As defined by CrunchBase, Twitter is "a social networking and micro-blogging service that allows users to post their latest updates. An update is limited by 140 characters and can be posted through three methods: web form, text message, or instant message."

In the software development industry, professionals move around, and Dorsey was no exception. His friends in the tech industry also use the whole gamut of communication tools: blogs, IM, text, and anything else that is current. Twitter was his solution for keeping up day-to-day with friends as if they were a bit closer in the universe. Because the messages are short, they can go out through any media, even iPhones.

Dorsey also successfully communicated with high-level executives in his field, as described in chapter 1, to advance Twitter. When Dorsey realized he had a great idea but needed to fully develop the technology and the exposure, he did not hesitate to reach out to tech industry legend Evan Williams. Williams had created Blogger and sold it to Google in 2003. Williams is even credited with creating the word "blog" and has been named as one of *Time* magazine's twenty-five most influential people of the decade.

A software developer engaging an industry legend with an idea for yet another social messaging technology: it was a bold and brilliant move on Dorsey's part, and it worked. With Williams and third partner Biz Stone, Dorsey founded Obvious, which became Twitter, Inc., one of the most successful tech ventures of the twenty-first century. Williams had the track record it takes to pull in tens of millions in venture capital dollars to make the product universally used. Williams had found out about the product initially from people in his company who were using it. With Ev Williams's name associated with it, Twitter went from a secret universe among techies to a popular way for people to stay in touch and, more recently, for companies to keep consumers updated on what is happening with their products and services.

Dorsey also had an opportunity to work through the principles taught in chapter 7, when his principles came into conflict with profit-making. He has always had a vision of what Twitter is and should be used for, and he has insisted on remaining true to that vision. In 2008, Twitter rejected an offer of $500 million from Facebook. One can only imagine the consternation of some of the venture capitalists who have backed Twitter for years. According to Portfolio.com, "As the service grew in popularity, Dorsey had to choose improving uptime as top priority, even over creating revenue—which, as of 2008, Twitter was not designed to earn. Dorsey described the commercial use of Twitter and its API as two things that could lead to paid features. His three guiding principles, which are shared by the whole company and through its culture, are simplicity, constraint, and craftsmanship."

With his ethics and his belief in the pure applications of his creation intact, Dorsey even got to experience the rigors of the moment of being fired, as we describe in chapter 6. You may not think that being moved from CEO to chairman of the board is the same as being fired, but in this replacement of Dorsey by Ev Williams as CEO, the industry saw Dorsey as being kicked upstairs.

Dorsey has been wildly successful in creating and launching Twitter; he pulled in venture capital money and made wise partnering decisions. He was at the helm when he got high-level national endorsements from actor Ashton Kutcher and

Oprah Winfrey. Still, he was removed as CEO. Just as chapter 6 recommends, Dorsey has taken the high road and has not played out any personal grievances in the media, social or otherwise. He remains one of the most admired people in the tech industry today.

JIMMY WALES, CREATOR OF WIKIPEDIA

How would you like to have more influence on knowledge and people's understanding on thousands of subjects than anyone in the world? How powerful is that?

Jimmy Wales has attained that position in our culture. Wales launched the open-content encyclopedia named Wikipedia in 2001. Because of his great influence on the way people access knowledge today as well as for his business acumen, *Time* magazine named him one of the world's most influential people in 2006. Like many electronic media success stories, Wales's monolithic success started with his desire to help a small group of people, students mostly, solve an information problem. Since no one wanted to be the coordinator of assorted information, Wales took on a job no one wanted, a formula for success that existed long before the Internet. As a team player, Wales demonstrates the communication strategies in chapter 5 admirably.

SARA BLAKELY, FOUNDER AND CREATOR OF SPANX

Sara Blakely started with a need, a need to create pantyhose to go under her cream-colored pants when she wore open-toed shoes—and she wound up with a huge piece of the two-billion-dollar pie called the hosiery industry. Blakely's success is even more surprising when one considers the strong male dominance in her industry.

But if you are thinking that she just fell into this windfall success that has led her to be a million-dollar contributor to Oprah's Leadership Academy and other worthy charities, think again. She was smart, did her homework, and was willing to rebuff the attitudes of skeptics—recommendations in several chapters of this book. Says Blakely on the Spanx website: "I read several books on trademarks and patents and researched pantyhose patents at the Georgia Tech Library at night after work. I then approached several lawyers who thought my idea was so crazy that they later admitted thinking I had been sent by Candid Camera. To keep costs down, I wrote the patent myself and later found a lawyer who helped write the claims. My patent was approved and I successfully trademarked the name SPANX online!"

Blakely also learned to talk to executives and get help from those who were ahead of her on the path to success, as described in chapter 1. She accepted seed money from Oprah. She took another risk when she left Spanx for three months to join the cast of the Fox reality show *The Rebel Billionaire*. For the show, she traveled all over the world with billionaire Sir Richard Branson. At the end, he handed her a check for $750,000; clearly, Blakely knows how to choose the risks to take.

BARACK OBAMA, FORTY-FOURTH
PRESIDENT OF THE UNITED STATES

The way Barack Obama handled his early career has a lot to do with his landing that very big job in 2008. Obama demonstrated skills described in four of the chapters in this book:

- His communication skills with peers and the powerful are widely documented (such moments are addressed in chapters 1 and 5).
- Temperament and coolness are hallmarks of the Obama style. He is an excellent model for the techniques for handling conflict described in chapter 9.
- Many people voted for Obama because they trusted him. Even in his early career, he was protective of his reputation for integrity, as recommended in chapter 7.

Even the Republicans admire Barack Obama's ability to communicate. He can give impassioned speeches about issues and inspiring addresses to rally support. But his ability to communicate one-on-one was more important when he was a young attorney. Whether he was trying to convince a federal judge of the merits of his case or arbitrate with one of his peers, Obama would approach communication quietly, thoughtfully. According to the *Chicago Sun-Times*, Obama was much more persuasive because he did not overpower adversaries with rhetoric or the power of his considerable personality. His quiet confidence and habit of working for, with, and through others contributed greatly to his success.

One of the most feared judges of his time was Judge Richard Posner, and the *Sun-Times* describes Obama's appearance in his court:

> *Only once did Obama appear before the prestigious 7th Circuit U.S. Court of Appeals, where Judge Richard Posner is legendary for tearing into inexperienced lawyers. But Posner knew Obama as a fellow senior lecturer at the University of Chicago Law School and kept his grilling polite. Obama never lost his cool, and he won the case.*

And the ethics and integrity needed by a successful presidential candidate are the same ethics and integrity needed by a successful businessperson, as laid out in chapter 7. The *Sun-Times* gives the following example of how Obama handled one early situation with integrity, as observed by a partner in his former firm, Judson Miner.

> *After three years doing "first-rate" work as an associate, Obama was elected to the state senate, and Miner offered to keep him on salary and let him open a Springfield branch of the firm.*
>
> *"He's such an honest guy. On the third day, he calls me up, 'Jud, I'm not going to have any time here, so I don't want to take a draw,'" Miner recalled him saying.*
>
> *So instead, Obama became "of counsel," working out of the office during the Legislature's summer breaks until he was elected to the U.S. Senate.*

SIR RICHARD BRANSON, BILLIONAIRE AND FOUNDER OF VIRGIN RECORDS AND VIRGIN AIRLINES

Some critics would argue with our adding Sir Richard Branson to a list of role models. But as an example of excellent communication with peers, subordinates, and the public, Branson is unparalleled. There are plenty of people who love him. And it is hard to argue with the success represented in over three billion dollars earned in a varied number of industries.

Many of the chapters in this book stress developing that type of diverse communication style, so Branson is an appropriate model for effectively dealing with others. The *Independent* article "Breaking Free: Branson's Early Years" (2006) offers this portrait:

> *Branson is nice to everyone who comes to meet him—even the cynics who consider him overexposed and shallow.*
> *He avoids saying "I," and only occasionally falls into the Margaret Thatcher trap of referring to himself as "we."*
> *And he is genuinely modest. He runs a Range Rover rather than a Rolls, and that's only because he was given one as a present. He leaves to others the uncomfortable job of firing staff who have outlived their usefulness. He is polite to the three secretaries who manage his overburdened diary. And when he flies to the States, he takes the bus into Manhattan along with the cabin crew.*

No one who knew Branson in his early years would have expected him to be a billionaire or to be knighted by the queen. He was considered an inferior student who often found himself in trouble for breaking the rules.

. . . Branson was initially expelled for his nocturnal visits with the headmaster's daughter. But, after writing a fake suicide note, Branson got the expulsion overturned. Back in school, Branson set up Student Magazine *at the age of sixteen and opened the Student Advisory Centre a year later, which was a charity to help young people. After his first issue of* Student, *the headmaster of Branson's school wrote a note saying, "Congratulations, Branson. I predict you will either go to prison or become a millionaire."*

In the next forty years, Branson would go on to prove his headmaster right on both counts.

The magazine led to a record store, which led to record producing, which led to an airline . . . Well, you get the picture. Richard and his friends went from one adventure to the next. If there has ever been an example of a collaborative management style, Sir Richard's is it. He has found the secret of making work fun and making business out of the things people call fun: travel, music, media, and so on.

JENNIFER HUDSON, ENTERTAINER AND ACADEMY AWARD–WINNING ACTRESS

You will notice that we don't call Jennifer Hudson a singer. She has become far more than that since her start on *American Idol*; she has become a major earning power in several fields. Hudson is one of the best models today of demonstrating how to be a winner, accept awards, and all the other skills described in chapter 10. She has won a Golden Globe, an Oscar, and a New York Film Critics Circle award. She completely stole the movie *Dreamgirls* from both Beyoncé Knowles and Eddie Murphy, and she is both respected and beloved by musicians, Hollywood, and Broadway. She handles her success and accolades with superb grace and poise. She is never arrogant but never diminishes her own personal power, either.

But her fans remember that for a couple of years Jennifer Hudson was most well-known for losing—not winning. With millions of Americans watching, she lost her position as a finalist on *American Idol*. In the equivalent of a Donald Trump "You're fired" moment, Hudson was ousted from the show, coming in only sixth.

Hudson demonstrated all the dignity and restraint we recommend in chapter 6 for the moment a person is fired. Can you imagine being terminated and then having to go on *Today* the next day and talk diplomatically about it? Hudson did it and did it well. She has since been invited back to *American Idol* to perform, and she does not disappoint.

Another sweet vindication for Hudson was beating out the 2002 *American Idol* winner, Fantasia Barrino, along with 762 other actresses for the role of Effie in *Dreamgirls*, and giving a performance that won her the Oscar for Best Supporting Actress.

And if her handling of both triumph and failure were not enough to convince us that Jennifer can teach us a thing or two about handling our emotions in public admirably, the way she dealt with the violent shooting deaths of several beloved family members certainly would. Although devastated emotionally, she represented her family and herself in a way that won not just the public's sympathy but also their respect.

What are some lessons you can learn from Jennifer Hudson, whether your career is in entertainment, transportation, human resources, or IT?

- Real life starts now. No matter how young you are, apply the principles in this book; you never know when an amazing opportunity could drop into your lap.
- Adversities, like being unjustly fired and being unfairly treated, will happen to the most talented people. Rise above it, weather it, and don't say anything you might regret when you have succeeded in your industry.
- Be a utility player. Be willing to do a variety of things to be successful. When you read the chapters in this book, some of the skills described will come more easily to you than others. You will be tempted to concentrate on those chapters. Focus just as much on the chapters that challenge you. Develop the abilities described and prepare yourself for success in a variety of situations.

THIS BOOK IS YOUR COACH

Eric Schmidt, CEO of Google, says in *Fortune* magazine, "Everyone needs a coach." Ideally, you have a coach or a mentor who can support you as you develop the ability to implement the strategies in these chapters with grace and élan. If not, use this book as your guide; the chapters have been written to lay out a clear path to success, one any reader can follow by putting the advice and techniques into practice, day by day.

Like any exercise that builds you up, practice and repetition strengthen you as you apply these principles on the job. And, just as when you work with any coach, you may eventually achieve success beyond the levels described in these chapters. You will discover new or better ways of handling people and processes and become accomplished in areas that go beyond this book. Then it is your turn to be the coach.

YOUR CAREER IS ONE-OF-A-KIND

Finally, take a close look at the title of this book: *10 Make-or-Break Career Moments.* The two most important words in that title are "career moments." Your career is different from any other career that has ever been. No one has ever walked your exact path with your exact set of traits, skills, and abilities. No one will have the same career moments or encounter the same cast of characters that your path will lead you to over the coming decades. So take all the knowledge and experience summarized in these pages and apply them, your way. Look at your situation with fresh eyes and see what applies; toss what does not work for your industry, your personality, and this unique passage in time in which you are building your career.

Use these chapters to prepare yourself for good surprises and bad ones in the workplace. You will have both. Use the wisdom drawn from the many sources interviewed for this book, but also use the initiative and instincts that led you to read this book in the first place. Dually armed, you will face the critical moments in your career with confidence and a bias toward success. The book gives you an edge. Your willingness to step out and try new things will make your career a success, based on your own unique definition of success.

BIBLIOGRAPHY

"17 People Who Changed the Internet Forever." June 2009. http://ittipsandtrics.blogspot.com/2009/06/17-people-who-changed-internet-forever.html.

Carmichael, Evan. "Breaking Free: Branson's Early Years." www.evancarmichael.com/Famous-Entrepreneurs/592/Breaking-Free-Bransons-Early-Years.html.

Dinardo, Kelly. "For Laid Off Workers, So Hard to E-mail Goodbye." March 5, 2009. www.usatoday.com/tech/news/2009-03-05-laid-off-email_N.htm

Drum, Brian, "Don't Accept that Job Offer Yet." August 8, 2007. www.military.com/opinion/0,15202,145310,00.html.

Dueease, Bill. "Eric Schmidt, CEO, Google says everyone needs a coach." August 20, 2009. http://findyourcoach.blogharbor.com/blog/archives/2009/8/20/4294691.html

Inglish, Patty. "Fired." http://hubpages.com/hub/Fired.

"Jack Dorsey." June 2009. http://cloudsonstreets.blogspot.com/2009/06/team-behind-twitter-jack-dorsey-biz.html.

"Jennifer Hudson." www.imdb.com/name/nm1617685/bio.

Lucas, Suzanne. "The 10 Questions You Must Ask After You're Fired." July 31, 2008. www.usnews.

com/blogs/outside-voices-careers/2008/7/31/the-10-questions-you-must-ask-after-youre-fired.html.

Maner, Kevin. "Short & Tweet." February 11, 2009. www.portfolio.com/executives/features/2009/02/11/Twitter-CEO-Evan-Williams-Q-and-A.

"My Pilgrimage to Omaha: The Great Warren Buffett Shares Personal Insights, Advice with Eager Group of HBSers." *Harbus*, January 23, 2006.

"Orrin Hudson Meets Donald Trump!" *The Chess Drum*, March 7, 2007. www.thechessdrum.net/newsbriefs/2007/NB_OHudson2.html.

Pallasch, Abdon M. "Strong, Silent Type: Obama's Legal Career." *Chicago Sun-Times*, December 17, 2007. www.suntimes.com/news/politics/obama/700499,CST-NWS-Obama-law17.article

"Richard Branson, The Brand." *Forbes*, November 26, 2006. www.forbes.com/2006/11/26/leadership-branson-virgin-lead-citizen-cx_tw_1128branson_slide_3.html?thisSpeed=15000

Robb, Bill. "Ask for their views upfront." July 14, 2004. www.trainingzone.co.uk/cgi-bin/item.cgi?id=128323.

"Sara's Story." 2010. www.spanx.com

"Twitter." 2009. www.crunchbase.com/company/twitter.

Walker, Peter. "Choosing the right path: Survey shows how MBAs plot their careers." CNN, July 24, 2006. http://edition.cnn.com/2006/BUSINESS/05/24/execed.career//.

Whitford, Josh. "Postcard from Warren Buffett." March 1, 2008. www.joshwhitford.com/2008/03/01/postcard-from-warren-buffett/

INDEX

V

Vacation, 63
Virgin Airlines and Virgin
      Records, 203–4

W

Wales, Jimmy, 199
Wikipedia, 199

ABOUT THE AUTHOR

Casey Hawley has served Fortune 500 companies as a communications consultant for twenty-three years. Her clients include Southern Company, Cox Communications, Georgia-Pacific, the U.S. government, and various nonprofits. In addition to her seminars and coaching for these companies, Casey teaches business communication for Georgia State University in Atlanta, Georgia. She is a National Endowment for the Humanities Fellow and author of five books by major publishers. Her previous titles include *Managing the Older Employee: Overcoming the Generation Gap to Get the Most Out of Your Workplace, Effective Letters for Every Occasion, 100+ Tactics for Office Politics, 201 Ways to Turn Any Employee into a Star Performer,* and *100+ Winning Answers to the Toughest Interview Questions.* Casey is also a contributor to *Chicken Soup for the Soul, III.*